International Series on Technical Innovation and Entrepreneurship

General Editors: George Kozmetsky and Raymond W. Smilor

Technology Companies and Global Markets: Programs, Policies, and Strategies to Accelerate Innovation and Entrepreneurship (1991)
  edited by David V. Gibson

University Spin-Off Companies: Economic Development, Faculty Entrepreneurs, and Technology Transfer (1991)
  edited by Alistair Brett, David V. Gibson, and Raymond W. Smilor

Technology Transfer in Consortia and Strategic Alliances (1992)
  edited by David V. Gibson and Raymond W. Smilor

The Technopolis Phenomenon: Smart Cities, Fast Systems, Global Networks (1992)
  edited by David V. Gibson, George Kozmetsky, and Raymond W. Smilor

The Technopolis Phenomenon

Smart Cities, Fast Systems, Global Networks

Edited by

David V. Gibson

George Kozmetsky

Raymond W. Smilor

Rowman & Littlefield Publishers, Inc.

ROWMAN & LITTLEFIELD PUBLISHERS, INC.

Published in the United States of America
by Rowman & Littlefield Publishers, Inc.
4720 Boston Way, Lanham, Maryland 20706

British Cataloging in Publication Information Available

Library of Congress Cataloging-in-Publication Data

The Technopolis phenomenon : smart cities, fast systems,
global networks / edited by David V. Gibson, George
Kozmetsky, Raymond W. Smilor.
p.   cm. — (International series on technical innovation and
entrepreneurship)
Papers presented at a conference held May 20–22, 1990 in
San Francisco, Calif.
Includes bibliographical references.
1. Information technology—Economic aspects—Congresses.
2. Telecommunication—Congresses.   3. Infrastructure
(Economics)—Congresses.   I. Gibson, David V.
II. Kozmetsky, George.   III. Smilor, Raymond W.
IV. Series.
HC79.I55T434   1992
363—dc20   92–10225 CIP

ISBN 0–8476–7758–3 (cloth : alk. paper)

Printed in the United States of America

™ The paper used in this publication meets the minimum requirements of
American National Standard for Information Sciences—Permanence of
Paper for Printed Library Materials, ANSI Z39.48–1984.

Contents

Part Two
Smart Infrastructures in a Global Context: Case Studies
of Trend-Setting Infrastructures

Part Three
Fast Systems: Technology Breakthroughs and Human
Resources to Accelerate High-Technology Development

List of Tables and Figures

TABLES

FIGURES

Preface

The Technopolis is an innovative approach to economic development that involves linking technology commercialization with effective public and private-sector initiatives to create new infrastructures for economic growth, diversification, and global competitiveness.[1]

The Technopolis Phenomenon presents ideas, programs, and initiatives that accelerate the creation of smart cities, fast systems, and global networks. It focuses on the development and implementation of an innovative and effective infrastructure for technology commercialization and economic growth necessary for global competitiveness in the 1990s.

The book's chapters were first presented at the conference "Attaining a Sustainable Global Economy: Linked Infrastructures—Smart Cities, Fast Systems, Global Networks," held on May 20–22, 1990, at the Mark Hopkins Inter-Continental Hotel in San Francisco, California. The conference brought together leading experts from around the world who were involved in creating, developing, and implementing the technopolis concept.

Part One provides an overview of key forces shaping the scope and direction of infrastructure development and implementation in the twenty-first century. Bob Hodgson uses the examples of Hong Kong, Singapore, and London to discuss the challenges and issues that underline global initiatives for technopolis development. W. W. Rostow relates the technopolis concept to the coming era of federalism, of large but not global groupings, within which the power of political and economic decision is divided in a hierarchy between central, regional, and local authorities. The relationship among technology, enterprise, and freedom is the theme of Chapter 3 by Regis McKenna. Part One concludes with David Alan Aschauer's discussion of the ways in which government policies may be directed to foster continued expansion in the global economy.

Part Two uses case studies to discuss smart infrastructures in a global context. Michael Wakelin describes Bechtel's experiences with technopolis projects throughout the world. The challenges to smart buildings in user-controlled ecological environments is the subject of Chapter 6 by Peter A. D. Mill and his coauthors. James Hudak describes the evolution of the multifunction polis concept using the experience of Japanese and Australian participants. Viacheslav Pis'menny concludes Part Two with a through-provoking description of future sites of high-technology development in the former USSR.

Part Three presents chapters on technological breakthroughs and human resources to accelerate the use of fast systems and the development of high technology. Frederick Williams discusses the concept of the intelligent network as it relates to the information infrastructure in the technopolis. Jerry Richardson discusses the important and often-neglected topic of management and training in information-based organizations. In Chapter 11, Sten Engelstoft uses the FAST program of the Commission of the European Communities to describe technopolis, cities and the human dimension.

Part Four is concerned with personal, institutional, and technological networks for infrastructure development and implementation of global networks. Howard Aldrich and Mary Ann von Glinow review key concepts to understanding the characteristics of personal communication networks and their relationship to infrastructure development. Stewart Brand describes how the technology environment of the twenty-first century will be so turbulent and surprise-rich that only fine-grained constant adaptivity will ensure sustainability over time. The case of Euro Park Alpha B1 in Germany is described by Gerhard O. Mensch in Chapter 14's discussion of European experiences and plans for EuroTechnopolis. Part Four concludes with Umberto Bozzo's description of the strategic choice of information and communication technology in Tecnopolis Novus Ortus, Bari, Italy.

The Technopolis Phenomenon concludes with Part Five and a discussion of strategic alliances for global economic development. Richard W. Morris focuses on the important topics of economic development, technology transfer, and venture financing in the global economy. Dominique Fache discusses the important and often-neglected topic of culture and entrepreneurial success as it relates to innovation in science parks. This book concludes with Sheridan M. Tatsuno's discussion of technology and the evolving urban landscape in the multimedia city of the future.

We believe that this volume provides both strategic and tactical insights into developing a new type of infrastructure for the twenty-first century—an infrastructure that contributes to enhancing the quality of life and the range of valuable opportunities in a global marketplace.

NOTES

1. For background on the technopolis concept see *The Technopolis Strategy.* S. Tatsuno, Reading, MA: Addison-Wesley, 1986 and *Creating the Technopolis: Linking Technology Commercialization and Economic Development.* (Eds.) R. Smilor, D. Gibson & G. Kozmetsky, Cambridge, MA: Ballinger Publishing, 1988.

Acknowledgments

Many people and organizations helped make this book possible. *The Technopolis Phenomenon* reflects their dedication to better understanding the relationships between technology and society, the evolving directions of economic development, and the emergence of new worldwide institutional relationships.

We are grateful to Ronya Kozmetsky, chairman of the RGK Foundation, and Cynthia Smith, director of administration and operations; Melissa Brown, executive assistant; and Jami Hampton, conference coordinator. The RGK Foundation provided valuable administrative support and organizational know-how for the conference.

We thank the following IC^2 Institute administrative staff, Chris Marcum, director of communications and administration; Ophelia Mallari, administrative services officer; and Rose Renteria, administrative assistant. We are especially indebted to Linda Teague, senior administrative associate, for her valuable assistance in seeing this manuscript from draft chapters to finished publication. The figures, tables, and format of the book have benefited from Linda's skill and hard work.

We are indebted to the sponsors of the conference, "Attaining a Sustainable Global Economy: Linked Infrastructures, Smart Cities, Fast Systems, and Global Networks," which was held in San Francisco, May 1990: the IC^2 Institute at The University of Texas at Austin, the RGK Foundation, Austin, Texas; the Bechtel Group, Inc., San Francisco; and Arthur Andersen & Co, San Francisco. The ongoing commitment of these organizations to research, education, and application made for a quality conference and the decision to publish the papers in this volume.

Rowman and Littlefield is a great press with which to work. We appreciate the interest and encouragement of our editor, Jonathan Sisk, and production editor Lynn Gemmell who helped guide our book manuscript to publication.

We are also grateful to the authors whose contributions made up this volume. Finally, each of us thanks his coeditors for making the work on the conference and the book such an enjoyable and productive collaboration.

Part One

Fast Forward to the Twenty-first Century:
Forces Shaping the Scope and Direction of
Infrastructure Development and Implementation

1

Technopolis: Challenges and Issues: A Tale of (at Least) Three Cities

Bob Hodgson

This chapter explores some issues that underlie global initiatives for technopolis development. The issues have emerged from work undertaken by our research team at Segal Quince Wickstead Ltd. in Cambridge, England and relate to several studies about global cities and technological development. A background review of technopolis development is provided and placed within the context of global opportunities and development dilemma. Illustrative material from three major cities—Hong Kong, Singapore and London—on which we have recently been working, is used to draw out some important messages. Concluding remarks place these messages within a broader vision of continuing urban technology development.

Much of this book is concerned with the global vision of technology-driven (or pushed) developments concentrated in world cities linked by sophisticated communications and integrated into a network of similar global centers that control and service an increasingly integrated world economy. I am enthusiastic about this vision, but as an analytical observer I see many challenges that must to be resolved. Accordingly, I will survey the subject rather than focus on a limited set of issues.

Language is the basis for most successful communications, so it is instructive to dwell on a some important words. Indeed, in view of the core role of knowledge in the information age, it is essential that at least the main parameters of the discussion are defined. *Technopolis* has been variously described, but its linguistic roots are in two Greek words: *technic* and *polis*. Respectively, these words originally meant "the study of art and the arts" and "the city," so logically, if not in common current parlance, technopolis is the city that pursues the study of the arts.

Common use of the word has replaced this definition within the notion of cities where the arts of science and the application of scientific knowledge are the driving forces of economic activity. Sometimes the word *polis* is varied and a substitute *pole* is used (*technopole*), which, coincidentally, is another Greek word meaning principally "pivot" or "axis" but also sometimes "sky." Hence, some of the fundamental ideas are contained in the title "technopole," a city of technology on which activities pivot. Also, some of the potential dangers are captured, such as the world becoming exclusively technocentric and an overdue concern for the sky, usually blue and virgin.

An illuminating story that captures the essence of the world scientific endeavor relates to how the "rediscovery" of ancient Greek learning contributed to the revolutionary period known in Europe as the Renaissance. Greek mathematics—including Pythagorean and Euclidean—was lost to Europe when Greece was overrun by the expanding Byzantine Empire. Fortunately, a group of Nestorian Christian scholars migrated to Gondisapur close to Baghdad, which at that time (eighth century) was a thriving center of Islamic learning. The Greek texts were translated into Arabic and the ideas were nurtured and developed through the centuries by Islamic scholars who followed the best open and inquisitive academic traditions.

In time this knowledge passed to the Arabic academic centers of southern Spain—Toledo and Cordova—where in the twelfth and thirteenth centuries radical (heretic) north European scholars such as Adelard of Bath and Robert the Scot came to study and translated the Arabic into Latin. Gradually these Latin texts found their way into north European universities and became the foundation for a renaissance of scientific inquiry that has led to many of the advances that underpin modern technological development.

In this chapter, several reflections on this tale are worthwhile. First, none of these historic cities, nor the cultures in which they were based, are currently world leaders as modern centers of learning or of technology-led growth. But a science park is being established in Athens, and science and technology parks do exist in southern Spain.

Second, sophisticated and culturally rich civilizations coexisted concurrently but independently during the period of the journey of Greek mathematics. These included China, India, and some of the civilizations of South America, but no equivalents existed in northern Europe or North America. A major difference today is the power and immediacy of international telecommunications, which can potentially merge cultures of the world into one accessible whole.

Third, the role of population movements in spreading ideas is crucial and the stimulus that can be gained from the transfer of people can have long-term effects. It is worth comparing the role and effect of higher education in the United States and the large proportion of non-American participants, some of whom stay, whereas others return home with their new knowledge.

Fourth, the role of culture is dominant in nurturing or repressing academic inquiry. The shifting nature of culture can change from supportive of open inquiry to repressive, and back again over centuries.

Fifth, international language plays a key role in storing and disseminating knowledge, as it did in the early days of Greek, Arabic, and Latin and does now principally with English. The task of scholars is to facilitate communications between nations.

And finally, unrelated world events apparently affect the whole process. Currently the world can benefit from the so-called "peace dividend," redirecting the financial resources released from the defense sector and particularly from the large corporate actors that play an important role in private R&D. It is worth noting that much of the impetus for leading-edge science and technology and R&D in both the United Kingdom and the United States arises from defense sector programs with their high-specification performance needs. At the corporate and product level there are important implications for the redirection of research programs and for the different relationship with clients who are likely to be more price sensitive. Major adjustments in pain and costs will be involved if such change is to succeed.

In large part the "peace dividend" follows from the dramatic economic and political changes which are surging through central and Eastern Europe. These changes are introducing interesting questions. Will Berlin reemerge as a global city of the highest rank? Will a new European bloc develop with a different center of gravity? Will this development further accelerate the breakdown of state barriers within the European bloc and is this compatible with the new nationalistic fervor?

THREE CITIES

Hong Kong, Singapore and London are only three cities that an informed group discussing global networks and world cities would include in a short list. I present these cities as cameos of particular characteristics rather than try to be comprehensive about each. I introduce other cities where their particular circumstances offer interesting contrasts and parallels.

Hong Kong

Hong Kong, a city of more than five million people, is an excellent example of the successes that can be achieved if the right climate for free enterprise is created and entrepreneurship is allowed to flourish. Hong Kong's original rationale was colonial dominance, with the drug trade located around the best deep-water mooring on the Chinese coast, but now the city plays an important political and economic role in the world.

The city's main characteristic is its regulated free market culture. It is crowded, hence land is in short supply, but so too are skilled people. The latter characteristic results in part from the political uncertainty facing the city and this shortage is causing production costs to rise among the 80,000 small firms. The dynamics of the area has something to do with the frenetic activity of the migrant worker with few alternatives, but it also is fueled by the example of the many who have remained and succeeded. In the short term there is money to be made, and the long term, which is about two years to Hong Kong businesses, can look after itself.

The immediate challenge of Hong Kong is to successfully manage the reabsorption of the territory into China. To maintain its global city status the city must attract higher-value activities—to revert to a trader/service center rather than to retain its recent manufacturing base. A key element is to retain its present current labor force and, where possible, to upgrade the technology content of its products and services. The opportunity exists for the city to retain its continued world role within an additional national and regional responsibility.

Hong Kong's development strategy, which is supported by private and public interests, is to provide massive infrastructure improvements and to facilitate technology upgrading. A new airport, at some US$20 billion, is a major investment and is backed by substantial additional transportation projects. On the technology side, there is to be a doubling of tertiary education to some 100,000 local places, which will still be only about half the number in the population in higher education. Part of this expansion is in a new University of Science and Technology with a planned 40 percent postgraduate population and 40 percent research content, both of which are completely new features among Hong Kong's universities. A new technology center is being provided with an important objective being to upgrade the technology competence of the commercial sector.

The questions that still remains are whether sufficient development and planning is being done and whether there is enough time left before Hong Kong reverts to China to create solid economic and knowledge bases. The long-term challenge is to channel China's scientific resources to encourage rather than to inhibit Hong Kong's development.

London

London is a global city of some six million people. However, the population has been declining for several decades as London's inhabitants have moved into the wider region around the capital.

London is a sophisticated and sometimes muddle mixture, a broad range of public and private enterprises, a truly multifunction polis. It has substantial concentrations of high-value and high-technology activities, including fifteen universities and polytechnics, some of the highest quality, with more than 70,000 students in the metropolitan area alone. But this concentration has not given rise to many R&D-based firms because there has been a shift outward to subregional centers. Oxford and Cambridge can be regarded as the natural technopoles of the wider London region, although the local communities would not recognize this description.

London's main challenge is shared by many long-established cities: to manage the upgrading of resources while continuing to play a world role. This is particularly the case in the producer services role for which the city is the global center. At the European level there are challenges to the city's role across many fields as the center of gravity of the community continues to shift eastward. At the national and regional levels the challenge is to manage the interconnected development of the whole region while not losing too many high-quality people to its satellite settlements that offer a better quality of life.

There is currently no strategy articulated for London's development, in part because of the lack of an overall body charged with the task and in part because of the city's influence across the greater southeast region of England. Dangers include underinvestment in refreshing infrastructure and the growth of diseconomies of scale. Some of these dangers are political and cultural, such as the reluctance to introduce road pricing to ration demand, to reduce congestion costs, and to access private capital to fund infrastructure.

Singapore

Singapore, an island city of almost three million people, is the regional capital of southeast Asia. Singapore originally developed as a port of refuge and a center for trade with China. The city developed to be a major trading center in the midst of resource-rich neighbors and now is an important regional hub with an efficient, high-quality image.

The main influence on Singapore is the dominant role of the central government. The city is well ordered and operates efficiently by dictate. Examples of this efficiency include the rationing pricing of city center road use and the computer-based control of port traffic. Controls are tight on all aspects of life, and an image attractive to corporate investment has been created. Within the past decade a radical move to restructure the city's domestic manufacturing base has been followed through legal moves to increase the minimum wage and invest in people.

Four challenges facing Singapore include (1) the maintenance of good relations with its larger neighbors; (2) the attraction and retention of higher value-added activity; (3) the emphasis on labor quality and skills, which also have a retention strategy; and (4) the introduction of flexibility into development, which is needed to attract the increasingly hybrid operations of high value-added manufacturing.

Singapore's problem has been attracting high-quality, high-value activities. Strategy used so far is creating the right conditions for inward investment, particularly for regional operational center functions. Concurrently, attempts to broaden the knowledge base have included upgrading various research institutes, investing heavily in both tertiary and advanced technical education and upgrading infrastructure and urban facilities. An opposite tack has recently emerged to develop collaboratively the adjacent Indonesian territory of Batham Island. This development extends the available land area and accesses a massive pool of low-cost labor for low value-added activities.

ISSUES AND CHALLENGES

Much debate rages about the concentration or dispersal of high-tech economic development and the related questions of centrality and peripherality. Stick to your competence, concentrate on excellence, agglomeration benefits are essential, and the only science that is worthwhile is good science; these ideas support concentrating on existing competencies and pursuing depth and excellence in scientific research. The converse arguments rely on the nonlinearity and unpredictability of scientific progress and the distinctive contribution that different approaches can offer—the spark of originality and the value of different perspectives. Both perspectives can be correct; the real issue is balancing the two. London is an example of the benefits of concentration applied to financial services but less so to science and technology, whereas an example of an alternative solution is the International Centre for Theoretical Physics (ICTP) and its satellites in Trieste, Italy and a proposal that Segal Quince Wickstead Ltd. has been working on for an equivalent center for mathematics in Edinburgh. Both centers aim to offer access for third world scientists to first world excellence.

In Europe concerns of regional cohesion across the community are strongly debated, and these concerns are echoed in the United States at the state level and in some parts of the technopolis strategy in Japan. At a larger scale, concerns arise in the relation of regional cohesion to the developing world and the consequences of a widening knowledge gap for a sustainable global development strategy. At the technopolis level the issue can become the emergence of city-states and regions with independent aspirations and the challenge that these operations raise to national development where the two aspirations may not comfortably coexist.

An attendant issue to centrality and peripherality is enclave, or integrated, development, which has several dimensions:

1. City life is unstable when two distinctive layers of inhabitants coexist.
2. Inefficiencies arise because of inertia in the system (the reluctance of Oxford to encourage commercial science development is one example).
3. Supportive and dynamic business and service networks are absent that ultimately provide the agglomeration gains of city living.
4. A separate breed of rootless people is created with an attendant instability because of a lack of commitment to place.

Penang, Malaysia, is an example where more than 30,000 jobs have existed in the electronics industry with major corporate players from Japan, the United States, and Europe working there for nearly two decades. However, no indigenous development has resulted.

MESSAGES

One major message from the examples of Hong Kong, London, and Singapore is that cities are complex places that offer a variety of supportive services and other benefits that have developed into a sophisticated and dynamic balance in response to their distinctive opportunities and needs. The multifunction polis of the major Australian-Japanese development (see Chapter 7, "Multifunction Polis: Partnering for a Global Technopolis") conveys some of this message. The challenge to all new settlements is to develop a distinctive identity that meets the diverse needs of their populations as well as creates sufficient value added to the world to prove successful. This value must result from the "functions" that are encouraged in the city rather than from the "shell" that is provided by the physical infrastructure. But the value must be sufficient to support the shell as well as the feeling that the shell contributes enough to warrant being provided and retained.

For the global city or technopolis even higher level demands must be met. These include the connections of the city with the wider world—its network of communications to other global cities and to its related (dependent) hinterland or region. This is the pivot or axis role on a larger scale and is typified by Hong Kong–China, Singapore–Malaysia/Indonesia, and London–United Kingdom/Europe connections, as well as their wider global hub roles. It is worth noting that the functional connection in the downward direction is at least as relevant to the efficient operation of the city as the higher-order outward connections.

A second message, which leads from the complexity and interconnected theme, is that world cities are regions. London most typifies this theme because of its dynamic but more sophisticated and established connections with the surrounding region. It takes more than two hours to cross the built-up areas whereas the United Kingdom's R&D concentrations of Oxford, Cambridge, and the western corridor of commercial technology toward Swindon are all within one hour's train journey of the center and are all within easy reach of an international airport. These are the technopoles within the London region, although the local and county authorities and communities, at least in the first two cities, have not risen to the challenge nor grasped the implications with unbridled enthusiasm. A significant part of this reluctance results from the different life-style, rewards, and demands of large cities and county towns and the awareness of the diseconomies of city living and working. The recent proposals for a regional city of Kansai in Japan echo this awareness of interlinkage and of the value attached to a high quality of life.

Another important message is the dynamic nature of the city scene and the constant requirement for the urban fabric to be refreshed. In established centers the will—political and professional—to institute the necessary upgrading and change is the issue, whereas in the new centers it is the creation of the circumstances in which the users and markets value the investment sufficiently to pay for it and provide an adequate return. The Exchange Square Complex in Hong Kong is an example of a "smart" building where the users value the image but do not use the high-tech facilities sufficiently to warrant their provision. In the literature on technology-related economic development, great emphasis is laid on the "champion," but in the complex city the challenge is the integration of champions into a forum or mechanism that enables a coherent vision of the whole to emerge.

As an economist—the professional who knows the price of everything but the value of nothing—I feel obliged to raise the often contentious questions of who pays and how? It is an almost universal feature (defense is perhaps the nearest to an exception) that technology is available to do much more than that for which it is currently used. In some instances, imagination and entrepreneurship are lacking to recognize and seize the opportunity. In many others it is the experience, and consequent aversion to the risk, that the market will not value a technological improvement sufficiently to pay the difference in the cost of providing it. One important lesson of the recent Japanese experience is that with the right competitive environment the level of embodied technology can be used to differentiate products and so create a competitive edge. So even here it is far from simple.

In relation to the technopolis and the often "public" goods of infrastructure and urban facilities the two main problems are how to capture the value created by the additional investment and "smartness" and how to ensure the value accrued to the party (private or public) that provided it, thus giving a return and a stimulus, if not the capacity, to reinvest. Road pricing is a particular question. Here, Singapore is closer to the answer than London even though the original idea for the central-area pricing scheme came from planning and transport professionals in London. Related issues of the costs and prices associated with dispersal and the historically lower tax on car use have helped shape settlement patterns across regions.

CONCLUSION

In this chapter, I have touched on a small number of the many fascinating questions that must be answered concerning the challenges and issues of the worldwide technopolis. In conclusion, I will mention a recent experience I had at lunch in one of the distinguished Cambridge colleges. I was excitedly discussing with a friend some of my experiences during a project to develop a science and technology policy framework for the Malaysian government when a young don joined the table and listened attentively. After a while he interrupted and said that he was fascinated by our enthusiasm but that the really important question to which he was devoting his academic life was posed more than 2,000 years ago and that he did not expect to discover the answer in his lifetime. I was too taken aback to ask him what the question was. But then it probably would have been all Greek to me.

2

Technology in the Coming Era of Federalism

W. W. Rostow

The title and theme of this chapter arose from the subtitle of the conference on which this book is based: Smart Cities, Fast Systems, Global Networks. It was the "global networks" that captured my attention. I have no doubt that the new technologies will not only continue to induce global networks, but they also will require global networks to realize their full potentials. On the other hand, I believe we are moving into an era of federalism, of large but not global groupings, within which the power of political and economic decision is divided in a hierarchy between central, regional, and local authorities. The emergence and refinement of these large federal structures—some tightly organized, others more loosely—are likely to be a central feature of the next half-century, perhaps giving way to an authentic global structure.

But there are fragmenting as well as unifying forces in the contemporary world; for example, they exist in reasonably civilized ways in Canada and Belgium, viciously and tragically in Northern Ireland and the Middle East, and in Romania and India and the former Soviet Union. The list could be extended. If nonsanguinary answers are to be found to this proliferation of regional conflicts, federalism again will be part of the answer.

In linking modern technology—its imperatives and impossibilities—to what one might call macro- and microfederalism, this chapter defines the special characteristics of the current technological revolution against the background of its three predecessors. Second, I define the forces of macro- and microfederalism, paying special attention to those forces related to the new technologies. Third, I identify certain problems in the diffusion of technologies likely to arise within macrofederal units, using illustrations drawn from Latin America, the Pacific Basin, and Eastern Europe. And finally, I draw a few conclusions on the potential positive role of the new technologies in relation to the federal process.

THE FOURTH TECHNOLOGICAL REVOLUTION

Major technological innovations tend to bunch. For example, in the 1780s they included the cotton textiles, Watt's improved steam engine, and good iron made from coke; in the 1830s, the railroad, which triggered the revolution in cheap steel; and near the turn of the century, the internal combustion engine, electricity, and a batch of new chemicals. The current technological revolution also has multiple dimensions: microelectronics, genetic engineering, new industrial materials, and lasers. One by-product is the revolution in communications. This technological revolution moved from invention to innovation in the mid-1970s. If history is any guide, this revolution may well last another half-century or more.

As compared with its predecessors, the fourth technological revolution has four special characteristics:

1. It is closely linked to areas of basic science, which are themselves in a fast-moving revolution. The scientific revolutions that underpin the new technologies generate an accelerated pace of innovation. These revolutions also require the scientist to join the team of inventor, entrepreneur, and worker. How closely the scientist, engineer, businessperson, and worker operate in partnership determines the pace of technological change in each society. It is the characteristic of the current technology revolution that explains why we all are here—because it explains the need for rapid communications along the whole spectrum from basic science to sales. It also explains the premium on the pace of innovation itself.
2. It seems fated to transform virtually every sector in the economy from the older basic industries (e.g., textiles, steel, motor vehicles); to agriculture, forestry, and animal husbandry; and to all services from education to military hardware, from medicine to banking.
3. Its new technologies are immediately relevant to developing countries, depending on their stage of growth and technological absorptive capacity.
4. It is so diversified that any one nation will not likely establish unambiguous leadership as Great Britain did in the cotton textile revolution or the United States did in the early days of the mass automobile. International competition will always exist, but the diversity of the new technological fields means that different countries will develop a comparative advantage in one or another aspect of high tech.

In this last characteristic we have the first link of the new technologies to macrofederal structures. While they encourage large regional groupings, as we shall shortly see, the new technologies also tend to limit the extent to which these groupings can rationally move to protectionism. Undoubtedly, those regional groupings will compete as Western Europe, the United States, and Japan now compete, but the diffusion of comparative advantage—along with the globalization of capital movements and of information networks—makes the emergence of a Fortress Europe, Fortress Pacific Basin, or Fortress North America unlikely.

framework. Now nationalism threatens international order and peace. A cool look at the contemporary landscape doesn't justify better than 50-50 odds.

The building of large federal regional units offers the best hope of creating a framework of order. Those who bear the responsibility in government or private sectors have every interest in helping build and support these regional units. Also, modern technology is both driving the world toward such large federal units and limiting any tendency they may generate toward excessive protectionism. But the dynamics of development has also yielded a proliferation set of schismatic subregional problems in many parts of the world with great disruptive potential, both locally and, even, strategically. One of the major tasks of large federal units is to devise solutions that permit aggrieved parties to share equitably in the larger adventures of federal units. The diffusion of modern technology can play a useful role in damping corrosive parochialism and reducing the likelihood of a world of Lebanons.

I conclude, perhaps above all, that the grand vision of smart cities, fast systems, and global networks cannot come to life if conceived in antiseptic technocratic terms. It can only come to pass if it is linked to and supports the coming political struggle for order rather than chaos in a world of diffusing power.

REFERENCES

Hume, David, 1758. See W. W. Rostow, *Theorists of Economic Growth from David Hume to the Present*, New York: Oxford University Press, 1990, pp. 29–31, 45–47, and 564–569.

3

Technology, Enterprise, and Freedom

Regis McKenna

".... precisely because technology is an extension of man,
basic technological change always both expresses our world view and,
in turn, changes it."

—Peter Drucker, *The New Realities*, 1990

The dialogue of technology with society is perhaps more obvious to us today than it was to our ancestors. We are more aware of ourselves as inhabitants of a rapidly changing world. We view and participate in global events through new and diverse communications. We buy goods with unfamiliar labels. We buy goods with credit cards. We push buttons and use machines more often than we used to. And behind these new gadgets, machines and new ways of doing things is unseen technology. Digital technology, in all its disguises, is the underlying engine of change. In 1960, there were fewer than 50,000 computers installed around the world. Today, more than 50,000 computers are sold every day. In 1975, there were 500,000 computers installed worldwide. Today, there are more than 15 million. It's little wonder that scientific knowledge is doubling every decade.

Today, citizens of the former Soviet Union and the United States exchange views by satellite on international television programs. An announcement made at the London Stock Exchange can reach Singapore in as little as two minutes. This instantaneous information transfer has made international boundaries transparent. Domestic economic decisions can no longer be made without regard to their impact on the rest of the world. More nations are realizing that isolating their economies (and their political systems) from international influences is virtually impossible.

Marshall McLuhan, the twentieth-century media philosopher, said any technology gradually creates a totally new human environment. And indeed, modern technologies are changing our total human environment. Technology is changing us as citizens of the world. It is changing our concepts of time and space and of choice and freedom. Actually, it already has.

It is characteristic of technological progress to make itself transparent in the sense that its social and political effects are not always obvious or measurable. It is also characteristic of technology to be influenced itself by social and political change. According to Peter Drucker, innovation is an economic and social term. Its criterion is not science or technology, but a change in the economic or social environment—a change in the behavior of people as consumers or producers.

TECHNOLOGY AS STRATEGY

As we near the end of this twentieth century, the industrialized nations, the newly industrialized nations, and the nations of the third world are keenly aware that the new electronic and biological technologies are the catalysts for economic, political, and social progress. Through technology, small nations that were once scraping by on their limited natural resources can now compete successfully with the established industrial nations of the world. Technological resources can leverage human resources, creating opportunities for everyone, rich and poor, big and small. Japan, Korea, Taiwan, and many other Southeast Asian countries are shining examples of this.

It is no longer possible to look at history and assume that the future will be a simple extrapolation of it. Technology is changing us and our world in ways that perhaps only future historians will chronicle with any clarity. Technology is creating a new world without boundaries.

Today, investment in technology is considered a strategic national objective. To grow and improve the standards of living for their people, more national governments are turning to technology investment. As a result, technology has become a powerful "political-economic" tool. A nation's strength is no longer measured by military might. In the latter part of the twentieth century, a nation's strength is largely defined by its GNP growth, its technology prowess, its percentage of world exports, and its competitiveness in world markets.

High-tech capital markets are now asserting their influence in national politics and economic policies. Governments are now competing with each other for new markets and a share of existing markets. They are investing to compete for capital, talent, new business enterprises, and wealth. This is why low-tax, limited government, deregulated, low-inflation, free-market policies are spreading globally. The same trend is driving us closer together, encouraging cooperation.

High-tech electronics and computing have transformed the world's capital markets into extraordinarily powerful economic and political forces as well. Electronically linked, operating 24 hours a day, and backed by advances in high-speed information processing and telecommunications, modern world financial integration ensures that money flows immediately to countries with the highest returns and best opportunities—national boundaries are ignored. As a result, capital is now driving trade. Capital market flows are fifteen times greater than are international trade and current account transactions.

The U.S. Treasury Department estimates that internation financial transactions of $200 billion per day, or more than $70 trillion per year, cross international boundaries. In effect, technology is creating a new economic global environment. To survive intensifying global competition, enterprises around the world are entering cooperative relationships. Cooperation is taking place through investment, cross-licensing, marketing and manufacturing agreements, product and industry standards agreements, component sourcing, custom design services, distribution arrangements, and even joint R&D projects.

Technology market forces are creating the competitive-cooperative paradigm. Ironically, in this new technocratic global environment, as the technological progress of any nation affords it a more competitive position in world markets, it must also cooperate more on business, technical, social, and political levels. To enjoy the fruits of new geographic markets, businesses must enter and become part of the political, social, and economic spheres of those markets.

Enterprises are turning toward their rivals to help them succeed in the new global competitive environment. Joint ventures, alliances and productive corporate relationships, unheard of twenty years ago, give businesses more economic and human resource leverage, shared capital cost burdens, and faster participation in new markets. Cooperation allows companies to access existing markets, gain knowledge of new and emerging markets faster, and potentially win larger pieces of that market as a result.

After its introduction, the telephone needed twenty years to reach a market of one million people; television, fifteen years; cable television, ten years; video-cassette recorders, six years; cellular telephones, four years; and personal computers, only three years.

Product design and life cycles are becoming shorter as a result of computer-aided design and telecommunications. In addition, the costs of research, product development, production facilities, and lost time are becoming burdens to even the wealthiest enterprises. Time compression is creating a greater sense of urgency, a necessity to act rather than to plan, to be engaged in the technology and the marketplace wherever it may be in a dynamic way. Time compression is causing more enterprises to explore ways to access technology and markets through cooperation. Competitors are finding it necessary to cooperate to meet the demands of their markets.

GLOBAL ENTERPRISE

Daewoo and Thompson CSF have formed a joint venture in ceramics. Motorola and Toshiba have joined together in product development, technology, and purchase agreements, and they jointly formed Tohoku Semiconductor Corporation. Sierra, Singapore Semiconductor, and National Semiconductor joined together to develop, produce, and market advanced application-specific integrated circuits. And there are many more such examples: Amdahl and Fujitsu; MIPS Computer, Kabota, and Toshiba; Syquest, Nippon, and Jafco; Benzing and Kanematsu; Zilog and NEC. In Europe, Philips joined with Thompson and Siemens to form the Joint European Silicon Initiative.

The technocratic countries of the world are forming a global Silicon Valley. Ideas are interchanged: chips from Japan and Korea, assemblies from Singapore and Mexico, software from France and the United States. Multinational sourcing, manufacturing, and marketing have become commonplace. About 40 percent of U.S. trade involves one branch of a company selling to another branch located in another country. Modern companies source globally, using the newest technologies from around the world and linked together by global networks.

Increased international interdependence is changing trade in another important way: The national origin of products is becoming harder to recognize. Technology businesses today organize their operations on a worldwide scale; their products cease to be truly American or Korean or Japanese. Parts, components, subsystems, products, and services are intermingled and exchanged. These trends are causing greater international economic integration and moving the world toward a true global economy.

The international nature of Sun Microsystems illustrates the globalization of business. Sun is a venture capital start-up established in 1982 in Silicon Valley. Sun is one of two companies credited with creating the engineering workstation computer market. The company grew to a worth of $1.5 billion in just seven years. Sun buys chips from Toshiba and NEC, uses Fujitsu to manufacture its next-generation miniprocessor, licenses workstation designs back to Toshiba, and then uses chips from other U.S. firms, which are fabricated in the Philippines, Japan, Singapore, and Scotland. And throughout, they use equipment made in Germany, Switzerland, Holland, and Japan. Such patterns of global interdependence are typical and essential to the high-tech industry. As more countries join the technological international trade arena, they too must join the global market system.

Choosing a product because it is labeled "Made in Japan" or "Made in the USA" is fruitless because so many products are made of components from nations around the globe. As the multitude of products becomes more complex, the unwitting consumer has few signposts to tell him or her much about the nationality of the product.

Consider the Ford Escort, the prototypical high-tech-produced car, which is made in Great Britain by an American manufacturer and contains parts from eleven countries. The Apple Macintosh, Sun workstation, and Convex computer are all multinational from a technology-origin perspective. Where should a consumer's loyalties lie?

Whatever the cause and effect may be, the global enterprise is addressing this new environment through massive telecommunications networks. For example, Digital Equipment Corporation operates one of the largest private global networks in the world. It has more than 41,000 nodes in 26 countries.

Another example is the Mitsubishi Group, an affiliate of twenty-eight "immediate family" members that include an oil company, a chemical firm, a steel manufacturer, and a bank, among other enterprises. This group is joined by more than 100 corporations with financial linkages. The extended family includes Nikon Camera, Kirin Beer, and many others. The Mitsubishi Group is investing $20 billion, to link thousands of enterprises over a global private network.

Yet, technology is not creating a common, undifferentiated world. Participating in the global economy means adapting to diverse markets and cultures. At a time in history when we talk of globalization, we also see the resurgence of nationalism. The nationalism of today, however, is not based on ideological politics, but rather on the demand for personal choice and freedom.

Technology creates the environment for choice because it has the capability to respond to the very environment that it has created. Technology markets are increasingly customer specific. Technology can tailor products and solutions to specific customers or groups of customers. This ability to address specific needs causes the fragmentation of the technology and the markets it is serving. True, technology markets are becoming global, yet they are simultaneously becoming more diverse.

Technology is creating this revolution in diversity of goods and services. There are more computer companies, more semiconductor companies, more software companies, more automobile companies, and more distribution companies competing in the world today than there were ten years ago.

"Other" is the leading producer of everything from textiles to cookies. Correspondingly, the markets for these products are fragmenting, not consolidating. Technology is the underlying force behind this diversification of goods and services. The tools of diversification are computer-aided everything, programmable chips, the computer, software, and telecommunications. These tools allow the development of products and solutions for narrower segments of the population or industry than was economically possible to produce before.

The consumers of the modern world have long been held captive by mass production—or lack of choice. Technology is not creating a more "common" world, it is creating a more diverse, interrelated world where choice is the primary value. The days of a uniformly accepted view of the world are over. Today, diversity exerts tremendous influence, both economically and politically. Technology both creates diversity and, at the same time, addresses the diversity of wants presented by society. As continuing students in this world of global awareness, we are educated to desire, demand, and expect choice and service because the world around us keeps producing examples of what is possible.

Economic levers will change as economies of scale give way to economies of knowledge and time. Users will play a greater role in the design of their own products and services as computerized manufacturing makes flexible production as economical as mass production. Technology gives production the capability for satisfying more and diverse markets as well as the ability to distribute and track thousands of new products in various markets.

In the United States alone, consumers demand and receive more variety and options in products from cars to clothes. More than 125 new consumer products are introduced every week in the United States. Automobile buyers can choose from more than 300 types of cars and light trucks, domestic and imported. Beer drinkers now have 400 brands to sample. The number of products in U.S. supermarkets has soared from 13,000 in 1981 to 21,000 in 1987. Such choice transfers power to the consumer.

This demand for variety, fed by technology and changing social attitudes, gives rise to new economic opportunity. Smaller nations are becoming stronger—becoming major players in the new world economy. Today, we see the rise of Singapore, Taiwan, Hong Kong, and other countries in the Pacific Basin. We also see the reemergence of many European countries, such as Spain and Italy. On the horizon, the emergence of Eastern European countries is being driven by economic reform and the need to participate in the new world order. There is no greater testimony to the interplay of technology, economics, and political structures as the events of the past two years in Eastern Europe have shown.

THE NEXT CENTURY

In the next few decades, we will see the emergence of many new powerful trading nations, perhaps countries like India or Brazil. The twelve-country European economic community is moving ever closer toward its 1992 target of striking down its economic barriers to become another major trading force on the global scene. But to be a prosperous economic community, it must ensure that the consumers and producers are not artificially separated. It must ensure that the dialogue of the global society and technology continue.

The next century will be the century of global transactions. Driven by the technology engine, it will create opportunities for new and old nations, both big and small. William Miller, President of SRI, speaks of the next century as the world century. It will not be a European century, it will not be an American century, it will not even be an Asian century. The twenty-first century will be a world century not by choice, but by necessity. Regions and nations of the world are interdependent and linked not only by trade and investment, but also by a larger number of problems that are transnational in character.

Technological change happens so quickly that our governments have trouble absorbing change fast enough to respond expeditiously. Certainly, technological change occurs faster than nations can change their bureaucratic structures. For the enterprise, as well as for nations, economic and technology positions will change quickly, and only the most flexible, adaptable, and cooperative will emerge as successful. Only those who think in terms of global linkages will evolve enterprises without boundaries. I believe that the global enterprise will and must take the lead in creating the superstructures and infrastructures of the global technopolis. Governments cannot.

The enterprise of the twenty-first century must be global. It must touch the people of the nations it operates within and markets to. To be effective, it must become a unifying force. Freedom is choice. Discovery of choice begins in the world around us. And in Marshall McLuhan's global village, technology brings the world of choice to the remotest of places. Freedom and technology are inextricably tied to one another. Destructive technology destroys freedom; constructive technology creates ever more desire for freedom.

Perhaps mankind has come to the brink in the twentieth century and has decided to put technology and enterprise to work to create a new global freedom in the twenty-first century. Perhaps the children of the twenty-first century will be educated by accessing a global, high-speed network. These children will experience, see, and interact with distant teachers and students. Strangeness, remoteness, and fears will crumble. The term *foreign country* will vanish from our lexicon. This world is not so distant. It is being created today by thousands of business enterprises while we speak.

4

Infrastructure, Competitiveness, and the Global Economy

David Alan Aschauer

We live in the springtime of a new global economy—a time offering the hope of renewal in the established capitalist world, of a full blossoming of the newly industrializing economies of the Pacific Rim, and of continued budding of the formerly state-controlled economies of Eastern Europe. This chapter presents the ways in which government policies may be directed to best foster continued expansion in the global economy. I assert that increased infrastructure spending—of traditional forms such as highways, airports, and water port facilities and of newer forms such as telecommunications—is one of the most important actions that the government can take to promote increased global economic integration—to help bring an end to a history of global economic and military conflict.

THE COMPETITIVENESS "PROBLEM"

It is common to hear talk of a competitiveness "problem" in the United States. Typically, analysts summarize the extent of this competitiveness problem by pointing to the sizable trade and current account deficits incurred by the United States during the 1980s. It is true that when a country becomes unable to produce and sell goods as effectively in the international marketplace and, at the same time, persists in maintaining a certain standard of living, its trade deficit will swell in size. By this mechanism, the citizenry is able to consume more than it currently produces. Over time, however, the discipline of the marketplace will dictate an adjustment in the international accounts; foreign citizens, after all, will not be willing to exchange goods for mere pieces of paper—various certificates of indebtedness—indefinitely. Thus, the surest indicator of national competitiveness is to be found not in any measure of the trade balance but rather in terms of growth in consumption possibilities, productivity, and export performance.

How does the United States stand in this regard? In 1986, per capita consumption in the United States equaled about $11,500. In the Group of Seven (G7) countries, our closest rival in supporting the "good life" is Japan, where per capita consumption amounted to $9,300, or 81 percent of that in the United States. In France, West Germany, and Canada, per capita consumption levels are roughly $8,000 and in the United Kingdom and Italy are between $6,000 and $6,500. Therefore, comparing per capita consumption levels in the United States with those in other G7 countries, we see that life in the United States remains good.

But it is important to distinguish between consumption levels and consumption growth rates; citizens of the United Kingdom in the nineteenth century enjoyed the highest standard of living in the world, whereas they now rank twenty-third among 142 countries—just above one of their former colonies, New Zealand. In this regard, the United States has not performed well of late. Over the past two to three decades, per capita consumption has grown more slowly in the United States—2.4 percent per year—than in all G7 countries with the sole exception of the United Kingdom (Table 4.1). At these rates, those living in the United States can expect to see their real consumption levels double every twenty-nine years, whereas Japanese citizens can anticipate such a doubling of living standards to occur in less than half the time, every fourteen years.

In 1986, the level of gross domestic product per laborer in the United States was 108 percent of that in Japan, 119 percent of that in West Germany, and 122 percent of that in Canada. But since 1960 the United States has seen a gradual, persistent erosion of its competitive edge. Average annual growth in labor

Table 4.1. Indicators of Competitiveness, 1960–1986, by Percentage per Year

G7 country	Growth in real consumption per capita	Growth in real GDP per employed person	Growth in real exports of goods and services
United States	2.4	1.2	5.0
Japan	4.9	5.5	11.0
West Germany	3.1	3.2	6.0
France	3.4	3.5	6.9
United Kingdom	2.0	2.2	4.1
Italy	3.6	3.7	7.7
Canada	2.8	1.9	7.0

Source: Historical Statistics, 1960–1986 (OECD).

productivity has been lower in the United States than in any other country of the G7 (Table 4.1). Japan, in particular, has achieved a productivity growth rate more than four times that of the United States, 5.5 percent per year as opposed to 1.2 percent. Accordingly, in 1960 the level of labor productivity in the United States was 333 percent that of Japan, 200 percent that of West Germany, and 147 percent that of Canada. Starting far behind the United States, without exception all the other major industrialized countries have converged on the superior competitive position of the United States in recent years.

Another indicator of the competitiveness of an economy is how attractive other countries find its export goods. A country with strong export growth must be doing something right in its productive endeavors. Japan's superior economic performance is evident in these export figures, with real exports climbing at a rather astounding average rate of 11 percent per year, more than twice that of the United States (Table 4.1). Only the United Kingdom, with export growth of 4.1 percent per year, has fared worse than the United States by this measure of competitiveness.

The data in Table 4.2 show how these differential rates of export growth have affected export shares of the G7 countries. Most notable is the 11 percent drop in the United States' share of total G7 exports and the nearly equal 11.4 percent Japanese gain. From 1960 to 1986, the Japanese export share has nearly tripled, from just less than 6 percent to more than 17 percent of total G7 exports.

The poor performance of the United States in export markets has spilled over into rising trade and current account deficits as well. The United States balance on trade in goods has been negative since 1974, precipitated by the oil price increases beginning in 1973. But because of its dominant position of economic strength after

Table 4.2. Relative Export Shares, 1960–1986

G7 country	1960	1986	Absolute change 1960–1986	Percent change 1960–1986
United States	33.2	22.2	−11.0	−33.1
Japan	5.9	17.3	11.4	193.2
West Germany	17.2	20.6	3.4	19.8
France	10.9	12.0	1.1	10.1
United Kingdom	18.9	11.0	−7.9	−41.8
Italy	5.3	9.4	4.1	77.4
Canada	8.6	7.6	−1.0	−11.0

Source: Historical Statistics, 1960–1986 (OECD) and National Accounts, 1960–1986.

World War II, the United States was at that time a net creditor in the international capital markets. Accordingly, for a time the income on our foreign assets exceeded the deficit in goods and, as a result, the current account remained in surplus. However, the current account swung from a surplus of $6.9 billion in 1981 to a deficit of $8.7 billion in 1982, worsening to a deficit of $154 billion by 1987 (Table 4.3). As the current account fell into deficit, foreign citizens began to accumulate more assets in the United States than Americans acquired elsewhere, and the net investment position of the United States started to erode. As a result, the net asset position of the United States—American holdings of real and financial capital in other countries minus foreign holdings here—peaked in 1981 at $141.1 billion; by 1985, the United States had become a net debtor to the rest of the world for the first time since before World War I. Indeed, while the citizens and government of the United States continue to acquire assets in foreign countries—U.S. asset holdings abroad nearly doubled between 1981 and 1987—foreign citizens have done so more rapidly. Foreign asset holdings here more than tripled during the same period.

This is not to say that foreign citizens are close to buying up the U.S. economy. As of the end of 1987, foreign direct investments—tangible capital such as land, commercial and residential real estate, plant and equipment, and the like—equaled $262 billion, whereas our national tangible wealth amounted to more than $14 trillion. Despite the fact that in Los Angeles foreign citizens own approximately one-half the available office space, in the aggregate foreign citizens hold a mere 1 percent of all real estate in the United States. In light of the aggregate statistics, the specter of the United States being taken over is just that—a specter. The United States won't become a second-rate power owned and operated by foreigners. At least not in the near future.

Table 4.3. Current Account and Net Investment Position of the United States, 1980–1987, in Billions

Year	Balance on current account	Net investment position of the United States
1980	1.9	106.3
1981	6.9	141.1
1982	−8.7	136.9
1983	−46.3	89.4
1984	−107.1	3.5
1985	−115.1	−110.7
1986	−138.8	−269.2
1987	−154.0	−368.2

Source: Economic Report of the President, 1989.

So eminent doom is not in store for the U.S. economy. Yet, along nearly all dimensions the United States has been losing competitive ground. What factors might account for this competitiveness problem? Ultimately, only by maintaining high productivity growth can a country sustain its international market share and effectively compete worldwide. But productivity growth, in turn, is most notably dependent on rates of national savings and investment. According to Martin Feldstein, a Harvard economist and former chairman of the Council of Economic Advisors, an increase in the saving rate is the key to a higher rate of economic growth and a faster rise in the nation's standard of living and the evidence is overwhelming that countries with high rates of saving and investment are ones in which productivity, income, and the standard of living rise most rapidly.

The two countries that have devoted the smallest shares of gross output to building up physical capital—the United States and the United Kingdom—are the countries that also have suffered the worst productivity performance in the G7 (Figure 4.1). At the other end of the spectrum, Japan's productivity growth rate of 5.5 percent per year is coupled with a level of gross investment equal to a remarkable 31.6 percent of the GDP. The linkage between investment and productivity holds up well across all the countries of the G7; quantitatively, a 1 percent increase in the share of output devoted to building up the physical capital stock boosts productivity growth by roughly 0.33 percent per year. As suggested by Martin Feldstein, this result has been confirmed again across a variety of countries.

So investment in new plant and equipment, by increasing the quantity and quality of capital goods available per worker, stimulates productivity. And productive efficiency is a key determinant of export performance. Thus, we should be able to find the proximate cause for our competitiveness problem in a low national investment rate. High national investment in Japan has been coupled with annual growth in exports in excess of 10 percent per year, while low investment in the United States has been associated with export growth of about 5 percent per year (Figure 4.2).

THE GOVERNMENT AND COMPETITIVENESS

What role might the government play in promoting international competitiveness? Most economists are quick to blame the government budget deficit for low national savings, investment, and output growth. Public-sector dissaving, it is argued, reduces the amount of funds available for investment in plant and equipment, which then impedes technological improvement and economic growth. It may be that an inflow of foreign capital offsets the public sector's profligacy, in which case the reduction in investment and economic growth is forestalled, but the negative consequence is then a deficit in international trade—the purported "twin deficits" of the 1980s in the United States—and a lower future standard of living as it becomes necessary to pay off foreign claims on domestic output. According to

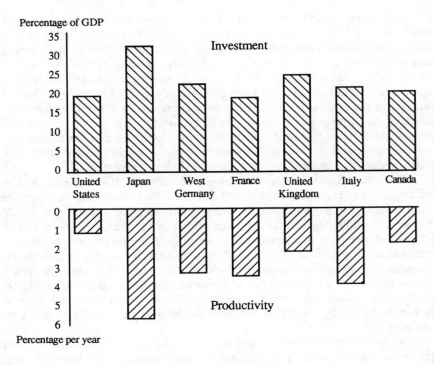

Figure 4.1. Investment and productivity, 1960–1986.

Harvard economist Benjamin Friedman, a prominent Keynesian, since 1980 we have broken with tradition by pursuing a policy that amounts to living not just in, but for, the present. We are living well by running up our debt and selling off our assets. America has thrown itself a party and billed the tab to the future. The costs, which are only beginning to come due, will include a lower standard of living for individual Americans and reduced American influence and importance in world affairs.

What is the evidence for such claims? From 1960 to 1986, all of the G7 countries have, on average, run budget deficits; they have been, on net, borrowers rather than lenders in domestic and international capital markets. While France has maintained near budget balance—an average deficit to gross domestic output ratio of less than 0.5 percent—Italy has incurred substantial deficits equaling about 6.5 percent of output. In between these extremes are countries such as the United States, with deficits ranging from 1.0 to just more than 2.0 percent of gross output.

According to the standard argument, countries that maintain high budget deficits should, as a consequence, suffer relatively poor investment andproductivity performance. This linkage is not readily apparent for the G7 countries

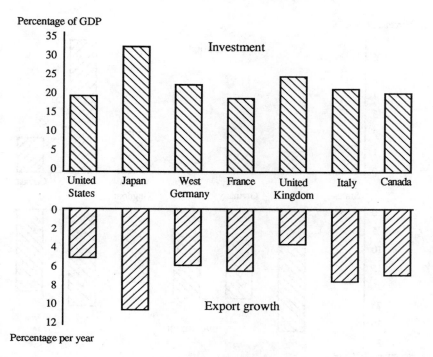

Figure 4.2. Investment and export performance, 1960–1986.

during 1960 to 1986 (Figure 4.3). While it is true that Japan has experienced lower budget deficits than either the United States or the United Kingdom and has had a higher rate of physical capital accumulation, it is striking that Italy, with a budget deficit ratio three times the size of the United Kingdom's and more than four times the size of the United States', has invested nearly 25 percent of output in physical capital goods. Overall, for these countries, there appears to be no correlation between government budget deficits and investment ratios; if anything, the correlation suggests a "crowding in" rather than a "crowding out" of capital investment by government borrowing.

The fact that investment and productivity are strongly linked leads us to be skeptical of the existence of any significant relationship between budget deficits and productivity growth. This skepticism is well grounded in the facts (Figure 4.4). West Germany's deficit ratio has been 30 percent less than that of Japan, 1 percent of GDP as opposed to 1.3 percent, yet the Japanese have achieved a productivity growth rate 2.3 percentage points higher than that of the Germans. Italy, with the highest deficit ratio of any country in the G7, has had productivity growth of 3.7 percent per year, well above the average for the major industrial economies.

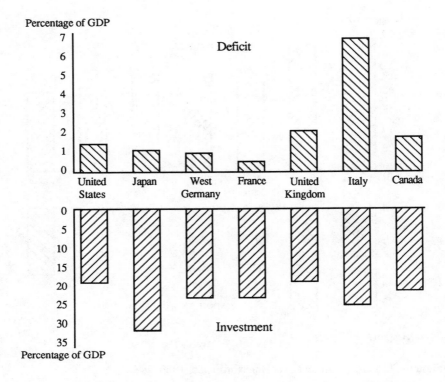

Figure 4.3. Budget deficits and investment, 1960–1986.

Finally, the evidence contained in Figure 4.5 yields little ammunition for the conventional argument that the budget deficit is associated with a current account deficit. Over recent years, Italy has achieved a current account surplus despite carrying the most substantial budget deficit ratio in the G7; the borrowing by the public sector has been financed through domestic rather than international resources. Whereas both Canada and the United Kingdom have incurred current account deficits and budget deficits over this period. Canada has had the smaller budget deficit and the larger current account deficit.

Advocates of the conventional position would put aside the evidence given earlier and would instead emphasize the relationship between budget deficits and trade deficits over time (as opposed to across countries). Representative of this line of research is Nouriel Roubini of Yale University, who presents results for the United States that seem to show a strong, positive relationship between deficits on current account and the general government deficit. But it is clear that these results caused by one episode, the ballooning of the Reagan budget deficits and nearly

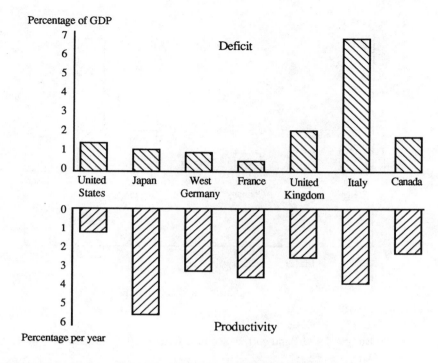

Figure 4.4. Budget deficits and productivity growth, 1960–1986.

simultaneous erosion in the U.S. international investment position. Indeed, the strong positive correlation between the two series from 1948 to 1988 becomes negative on deletion of the years after 1983 from the sample. Not only that, but the Roubini result is not statistically robust; William Dewald and Michael Ulan of the U.S. State Department pointed out some statistical problems with his work and, upon making the appropriate corrections, concluded that there is no statistically significant relationship between the general government deficit and the U.S. current account deficit. Moreover, the estimated coefficients in the corrected equation are much smaller in absolute value than Roubini's.

Even if we were to accept the positive relationship between budget deficits and the current account in the United States, in many other countries the data do not conform to the same pattern. Eduardo Borensztein of the International Monetary Fund looked at a wide sample of 30 countries and found an almost even split between countries which show a positive correlation between fiscal deficits and current account deficits and countries which show a negative association. Examples of the latter result are not difficult to find. The British public-sector budget deficit was 3 percent of GDP in 1981 and swung into surplus by 1988; yet during the same years the United Kingdom's current account passed from a surplus of 3

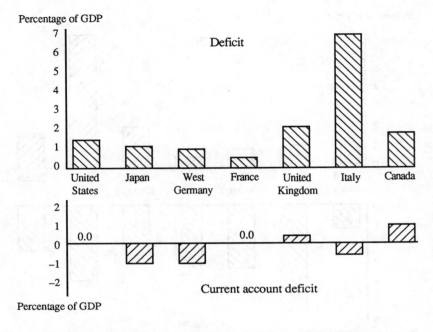

Figure 4.5. Budget deficits and current account deficits, 1960–1986.

percent of output to a deficit of equal magnitude. Outside of the G7, Denmark had a budget deficit of 9 percent of gross product in 1982 and a current account deficit of 4 percent; but by 1986, the budget was in surplus equal to 3 percent of output and the current account deficit had actually increased.

Although it may be claimed that other factors are responsible for these "bizarre" results, the same can be said with respect to the "twin deficits" of the United States. Indeed, we may cite a few possible reasons—other than the budget deficit—for the fall-off in U.S. domestic savings and associated current account deficits after 1982. First, the stock market boom beginning in that year and increases in residential real estate values have worked to increase wealth and, thereby, to reduce the need to add to wealth—accomplished via savings. Second, the majority of members of the post-World War II "baby-boom" generation reached a high spending age—from 16 to 35—in 1980. The bottom line is that America's challenge is not just to cut its budget deficit but also to increase private savings.

This focus on other potential causes for a low private and national savings rate leads to specific policy initiatives to boost the national savings rate, as well as to spur private capital accumulation. Such policy proposals bandied about in Washington from time to time include consumption-based tax systems, individual retirement accounts, preferential tax treatment of long-term capital gains, accelerated depreciation of physical capital assets, and investment tax credits. And although economists quibble about the quantitative importance of these savings and investment incentives, they are in near unanimous agreement on their qualitative significance for economic growth and competitiveness.

However, there is another potential "supply-side" avenue by which public policy can influence the process of economic expansion. What the entries in the list of policies mentioned earlier have in common is that they work through the tax system to affect either the supply of loan funds—savings—or the demand for those funds—private investment in capital goods. Instead, we might look to the opposite side of the government's budget—the composition of public expenditure and the possible effects various budget policies may have on private-sector productivity and national competitiveness.

Specifically, we may differentiate between public-sector consumption and public-sector investment and argue that this distinction is as important for economic growth calculations as is the analogous calculation on the private side of the economy. Public investment in a basic infrastructure of roads, highways, mass transit, airports, port facilities, and similar structures has two important effects on private-sector production, productivity growth, and competitiveness. The first effect on private output growth arises from the availability of public capital to support private-sector production; roads, highways, and airports allow the distribution of goods and services throughout national and international markets. Indeed, a close correspondence between public investment in nonmilitary capital and productivity growth exists across the G7 countries (Figure 4.6). Japan, which spends in excess of 5 percent of its output on its nonmilitary public capital stock, has achieved productivity growth in excess of 3 percent per year; at the other end of the spectrum is the United States, with low public investment at less than 2 percent of output and consequent low productivity growth. A detailed statistical analysis of the connection between investment in infrastructure and productivity growth across these countries indicates that an increase of 1 percent in the ratio of public investment to output brings about a rise in annual productivity growth of about a 0.33 percent, this is about the same as the effect of private investment on productivity.

The second effect of infrastructure spending on the economy arises from the complementarity between private and public capital in producing private-sector goods and services. Private plant and equipment work side-by-side with public transportation facilities, water and sewer systems, and other elements of the infrastructure to generate and deliver goods and services to national and international markets. Whereas private capital may be the heart of the body economic, public-sector capital acts as its arteries, carrying life's blood to its ultimate uses.

What this implies is that an increase in public-sector capital tends to raise the profitability of private plant and equipment and, over the space of several years, tends to spur additional private investment. Rather than crowding out private investment, public investment crowds in private expenditure on machinery and plant, thereby elevating the national—public plus private—level of capital

Percentage of productivity growth

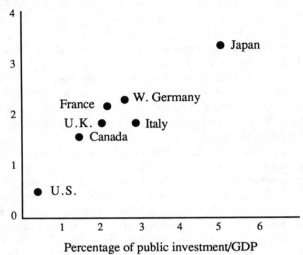

Percentage of public investment/GDP

Figure 4.6. Percentage of public investment and productivity.

accumulation. For example, a country like Japan with a high level of public investment also has a lofty level of national investment as opposed to a country like the United States, with a government budget biased toward public consumption and away from public investment that also suffers from low private investment (Figure 4.7).

Putting the pieces of the argument together, then, our competitiveness in international markets depends crucially on our productive efficiency which, in turn, is largely determined by our overall propensity to save and invest in new capital. Public investment, by directly raising productivity as well as by promoting private investment, works doubly hard to enhance our worldwide competitive position.

CONCLUSION

So we see that from the standpoint of national budget policy, perhaps the most important consideration for a country's competitive position is not with the budget deficit—the excess of spending over tax revenue—but rather with the way the government spends its money. After all, while the Japanese economy has been outperforming that of the United States, the Japanese government debt burden—measured as the public debt as a percentage of gross domestic output—has been much higher than that of the United States; in 1985, the Japanese public debt

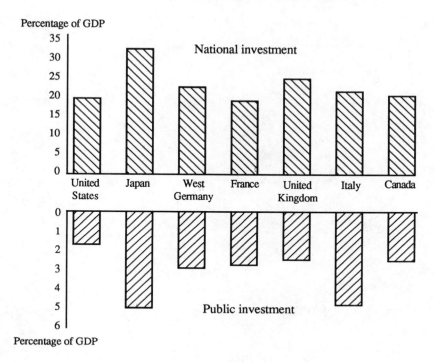

Figure 4.7. Public investment and national investment, 1960–1986.

amounted to 55 percent of GDP, compared to 39 percent in the United States. Budget deficits may be partly responsible for our own and other nations' economic difficulties, but by focusing on the potential link between public-sector deficits and the trade deficit, we gamble on ignoring the direct, observable link between the state of our infrastructure and the health of the domestic and global economy. It would be blindness, indeed, if the United States as a nation were to opt to balance the budget by slashing public investment in infrastructure, in the network that binds us to the ever-blooming global economy.

Part Two

Smart Infrastructures in a Global Context:
Case Studies of Trend-Setting Infrastructures

5

Globalization of Regional Development

Michael Wakelin

It has now been a decade since MITI announced its regional technopolis concept as part of Japan's "Vision for the '80s." What has been learned about the technopolis experience to date, and where is the concept going?

Bechtel's perspective is that of a company that, although a relative newcomer to the technopolis dialogue, has in fact been in the business of developing new communities and major infrastructure links for a good part of this century. Bechtel's participation in planned new communities goes back more than twenty-five years, including the seaport industrial city of Jubail in Saudi Arabia, which has been listed as the largest construction program in the world. Elsewhere, Bechtel has participated in the planning and implementation of major infrastructure links, notably the tunnel link between the United Kingdom and France and the strategic highway under construction across Turkey (and continuing in the direction of the Persian Gulf). Currently, Bechtel is participating in projects on both sides of the Strait of Gibraltar.

At first glance, the Japanese vision of technopolis and the Bechtel history of megaprojects look worlds apart: one represents the cutting edge of high technology and its glitter, the other is the expression of the megaproject, with its emphasis on resource-based industries and heavy infrastructure. And yet, one can find in these past and more traditional projects some valuable lessons for successful technopolis development, including

- The need to locate advanced infrastructure in strategic regions
- The need to see a project as a link between its region and activities elsewhere in the world
- The need to reconcile local and regional concerns with a global vision.

The key to the next phase of technopolis will be to integrate these themes into the growing movement of building new technology-based communities. We have begun doing this in a variety of projects around the world.

Bechtel's first technopolis project was to prepare a master plan to extend the Centro Studi Applicazioni Novus Ortus Avanzate (CSATA) technopolis facilities in Bari, Italy, and the company's involvement in this project continues to this day. Currently, Bechtel has more than ten technopolis projects under way in France, the former Soviet Union, Morocco, Thailand, Japan, and the United States. Bechtel has also contributed to the bilateral Japanese–Australian Multifunction Polis (MFP) with great interest.

Of particular interest over the past decade has been development of the airport city concept, the high-tech hub of the future. Together with Bechtel's aviation arm, the project development group is playing an increasingly important role on such airport projects as the Aeropolis program in Chitose/Sapporo, Japan, and the airports in Hong Kong; Seoul/Inchon, Korea; Kansai, Japan; and the United States.

The technopolis programs that are evolving in each of these regions can be described from many perspectives. We envision an encircling privatized global infrastructure network creating conditions for accelerated development of the knowledge-based market economy in strategic regions. Critical elements of the globalization of regional development are shown in Figure 5.1. An integrated fast system of technology transfer is replacing the outdated, technology-starved public sector developed earlier in this century. It is our expectation that infrastructure based on advanced technology will create conditions for dynamic development. This we call Dynapolis,[1] the city–state of the future.

The Second International Technopolis Conference, held in San Francisco in 1990 and sponsored in part by Bechtel, gave us an opportunity to share some of our experience and to ponder with our colleagues where we are going. It provided participants an excellent forum to discuss the activities, programs, strategies, and projects associated with the technopolis phenomenon over the past twenty years, going back to the beginning of the French Technopolis Program in 1969.

The conference proceedings provide a synthesis of the major ideas and concepts concerning the development of technopolis and show the various perspectives of the authors.

INFRASTRUCTURES

In the 1890s, the economy of Great Britain, the first global power, was based on a slow system of east-west sea lanes, connecting defensible strategic locations around the world from London to Gibraltar, Malta, Suez, Aden, and Colombo, to Singapore, Hong Kong, and the Far East. A southern route around the Cape of Good Hope tied Africa and Asia to the industrializing island state. The primary function of the infrastructure system was to import bulk natural resources and export manufactured goods. Equally important was the communication system required to administer and develop the economic activities of a widely diffused and dispersed empire. For its time, the infrastructure system of the empire was the fastest and smartest, incorporating the most advanced technology of the last quarter of the nineteenth century. In the twentieth century, things have changed:

> The central event of the twentieth century is the overthrow of matter. In technology, economies and policies of nations, wealth, in the form of physical resources, is steadily declining in value and significance. The powers of mind are everywhere ascendant over brute force of things. . . . This change marks a great historic divide. Dominating previous human history was the movement and manipulation of massive objects against friction and gravity.[2]

Originally, "infrastructure" referred to the support system of the military, (e.g., Roman roads, city walls, and moats). Today, privatized infrastructure is encircling the world, freed from the monopolistic, moribund hand of government, and becoming faster and smarter. At the crossroads or linkages of the new infrastructure, dynamic strategic regions will emerge. Within this regional infrastructure framework, as the influence of nation–states recedes and supranational alliances expand, the global city will arise. The terms *technopolis* (or *technopole*) and *multifunction polis* (MFP) are used to describe the phenomenon; at Bechtel, the term *Dynapolis*, the city–state, is used.

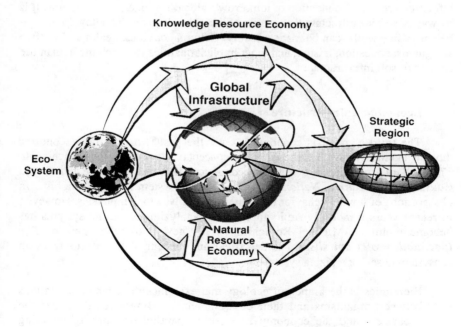

Figure 5.1. Globalization of regional development.

TYPES OF INFRASTRUCTURES

Infrastructure is usually regarded as a public-sector, nonproductive category of the economy. In the context of this discussion, infrastructure is seen as a comprehensive three-tier integrated system comprising hard, soft, and economic elements organized into a privatized market economy.

Hard Infrastructure

The hard infrastructure consists of all systems of conveyance for people, products, raw materials, and communications. It includes the networks of air and surface transportation, ports, airports, terminals, canals, pipelines, highways, railroads, cableways, subways and elevators; storage and distribution systems of water; power generation and transmission lines; gas and oil networks; the treatment systems for all forms of waste; and all aspects of telecommunications.

Soft Infrastructure

The soft infrastructure comprises education and governance. This infrastructure is the foundation of tomorrow's global fast interactive systems. It is by way of soft infrastructure that quality of life—the elements that allow for human beings to live well—can be made a reality. Cultural activities, health and welfare safeguards, education, leisure, and other implicit qualities to enrich the human life are part of soft infrastructure.

Economic Infrastructure

The third element is economics. Over the past two centuries, economic thought and theory have been based on the concept of the economy as a machine. In 1776, Adam Smith, in his treatise on economics, *An Inquiry into the Nature and Causes of the Wealth of Nations*, described a static system derived from his own observations of human behavior (self-interest) and Newtonian physics. However, in recent years a more dynamic approach to analyzing economic systems has become common. Michael Rothchild, in his new book, *Bionomics—The Inevitability of Capitalism*, has described his concept of the economy as an ecosystem (a self-organizing system):

> Bionomics is the branch of ecology that examines the economic relations between organisms and their environment. . . Bionomics describes the ecosystem and the economy as separate parallel domains of evolving information. Genetic information, recorded in the DNA molecule, is the basis for all organic life. Technical information, captured in books, blueprints,

scientific formulas, databases and the know-how of millions of individuals is the source of all economic life . . . and remarkably neither the global ecosystem nor the global economy needs a conscious force to keep it organized.[3]

It follows that design of the global infrastructure and its interface with the ecosystem must be understood as an organic and evolving phenomenon.

THE STRATEGIC REGION

Until recently, strategic regions were thought of more as potential flashpoints between nations rather than areas of economic opportunity.[4] They have been seen as zones of conflict—witness the recent Persian Gulf War in a region containing 40 percent of the world's oil reserves. Another way of looking at such regions is to interpret them as points of linkages, geoeconomic bridges, that are key to the process that gives rise to an interdependent global market.

There are five types of strategic regions, each characterized by a dominant infrastructure system:

1. Seaport gateway regions
2. Corridor (landbridge) regions
3. Interior "pole" regions
4. Airport hub regions
5. Transnational region (Figure 5.2).

Seaport Gateway Regions

Port cities and their regional hinterland are the most typical strategic region. This has been particularly true during the historic and current industrial era. New York, London, and Shanghai were centers of trade, power, and wealth. The port functions and cluster of various international terminals were the focus of

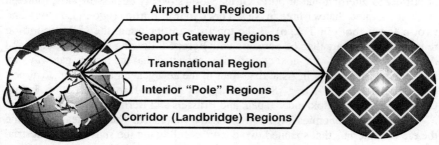

Figure 5.2. Strategic regions.

international trade. As historic functions have declined, modern facilities have been developed at deep-water integrated industrial complexes, such as Rotterdam, Singapore, and Jubail in Saudi Arabia. The original London Docklands area is today Europe's largest redevelopment project, including, significantly, a STOL airport.

Corridor (Landbridge) Regions

The infrastructure linear distribution systems were built in parallel to follow the landform lines of least resistance. They connected coast-to-coast across both water and land and opened paths to the interior, primarily to extract natural resources (e.g., coal and copper). The primary function was to move bulk goods inexpensively.

Interior "Pole" Regions

Most trading cities were developed on the waterfront of oceans, lakes, and rivers. In this century, capital cities have been created in the interior of several countries (e.g., Canberra in Australia, Ankara in Turkey, Brasilia in Brazil, Islamabad in Pakistan, and Abuja in Nigeria). These cities were built to accelerate growth in the interior and to offset the economic power of coastal regions. Future interior strategic regions may center on Berlin, Germany, on a new capital for Japan, and on Brussels as capital of the EEC. In the United States there has been a notable change in what were sleepy state capitals. Austin, Texas; Columbus, Ohio; and Sacramento, California, are examples of technology and cultural clustering.

Airport Hub Regions

Obviously, there are no historic examples of airport cities, but we have witnessed the growth of the knowledge-based economy and its dependence on proximity to international airports. Of the world's twenty busiest airports, fourteen are in the United States (three in New York), four in Europe (two in London), and two in Japan (both in Tokyo). If the top fifty are included, the U.S. proportion remains high at more than 60 percent, with Europe following with 25 percent, and Asia at 10 percent. In the next century, it is expected that the airport gateway city will evolve, particularly in Asia. Examples of the new generation of planned airport cities include Hong Kong, Seoul/Inchon in Korea, Kansai/Osaka in Japan, Chitose/Sapporo in Hokkaido, Japan, and Brussels and Berlin in Europe.

Industrial economies have now reached a watershed. They are leaving behind the era of materials that spanned two centuries following the start of the industrial revolution and are moving into a new era in which the level of material use will no longer be an important indicator of economic progress. In the United States, steel consumption in the national economy, as measured by kilograms per unit of GNP, is roughly what it was 100 years ago, down from its peak in 1920.[5] California has already entered the era of information and of smart materials. More than 50 percent of California exports, by value added, leave the state by air, and the state is now sixth in the ranks of nation–states.

Transnational Region (The Global Bridge)

New strategic regions are most likely to emerge in areas that lie across national boundaries, particularly at a junction of three or more countries. One such example is the Channel Region within the triangle of London, Paris, and the new European "capital" Brussels. Currently under construction is the $15 billion tunnel complex between the United Kingdom and France. The short-term effect will be to stimulate double the investment in infrastructure development—the TGV (high-speed train), new ports, airports, and railroad terminals in London; Brussels; Lille, France; Ashford, United Kingdom; and beyond. A Lille location will serve three major cities and be at the hub of new ports and airports. Other examples of "missing linkages" are those to Africa (Strait of Gibraltar), to the Persian Gulf through Turkey, and to the former Soviet Union via Berlin and Anchorage, Alaska.

In the Far East, other strategic regions could emerge, particularly around the Sea of Japan (Korea, the People's Republic of China, the former Soviet Union, and Japan) or between Taiwan, Macao, Hong Kong, and the People's Republic of China, or in the Singapore-Malaysia-Indonesia triangle.

Each region must invest in its integrated infrastructure systems if it is to be linked profitably to other global regions. Regions that make such investments will enhance their global position and their competitive advantage. Bangkok could exploit its Europe-Asia global bridge location and compete with Singapore. Hokkaido and Anchorage could establish links with the resource-rich regions of the eastern part of the former Soviet Union. Hong Kong could become the economic capital of China, overshadowing the Shanghai and Beijing regions.

All the strategic regions will derive competitive advantage from being open, free (democratic), and with a market economy (capitalist). This will also hold true for other regions that wish to compete in the global strategic sweepstakes.

The next century will not be the Pacific Century, nor will it witness a return to European predominance; it will be the Global Century. The first step will be the globalization of regional development and the emergence of the global city, Dynapolis. Trade, science, culture, and geopolitics have much farther to travel to the Global Century. Few of the present Fortune Global 500 corporations are truly global; they are, in reality, large nation-based corporations—at best, multinational companies.

Technopolis could be a name for a science campus or a new science city or a metropolitan diffusion of global functions. For some, it is ectopia, the technology-linked, invisible city of the mind. But already technopolis signals the death of the industrial town of mass repetitive production, the decline of the port city, and the revival of the culture of cities in general. John Naisbitt sees "this megatrend of the next millennium (a new electronic heartland of linked small towns and cities) as laying the groundwork for the decline of cities."[6] He also states that "in many ways, if cities did *not* exist, it now would not be necessary to invent them,"[7] and that the "truly global cities will not be the largest, they will be the smartest."[8]

THE CHALLENGE

City Autonomy

A new culture of cities must be created, and they must regain their autonomy.

Historically, cities were able to control their development and thus were thought of as culture but, with the rise of the nation states, they lost most of their autonomy and were overwhelmed by the accelerating rates of industrialization, urbanization, and population growth. . . The metropolis is not a city unless it is self-governing. This is an historic period: cities are now able to position themselves in the global society. Human settlements from historic cities to megacities are at a crucial *crossroads*: they can either participate in shaping the global society or they can react to global forces and be shaped by them.[9]

Infrastructure Investment

Infrastructure must be transfused with modern technology, thereby adding value and making infrastructure profitable and part of the productivity equation. Infrastructure must be made global, fast, and smart.

A Regional Agenda

A global regional agenda must be discovered. Regional development is typically a contentious local affair. The typical agenda is focused on pollution mitigation, eliminating traffic congestion, and growth control. What is lacking is an external focus that binds regional self-interest into a global strategy.

THE RESPONSE—A FIVE-STEP PROCESS

Determining strategies for the globalization of regional development comprises five major steps (Figure 5.3). It begins with an exploration of the assets that give the region global significance and culminates in the development of a global implementation strategy. The strategy addresses costs, schedules, financing, and markets and identifies potential participants in projects. The product is a program of projects to create a Dynapolis supported by viable, linked-infrastructure projects.

1. *The Strategic Region.* Determine which assets qualify a region as strategic to the world economy and determine their potential for supporting regional growth.
2. *Global Linkages.* Assess the region's existing global linkages, and identify the potential new linkages required to participate in the global network.
3. *Infrastructure Integration.* Identify the opportunities for integrating the new linked infrastructure, determine its place in regional and national development, and identify megaprojects.
4. *Economic Opportunity.* Create a global city, a Dynapolis, to provide the advanced urban hard and soft infrastructures to support the new economic development process.
5. *Global Implementation Strategy.* Develop a global implementation and marketing strategy through partnering with potential participants—governments, corporations, and institutions.

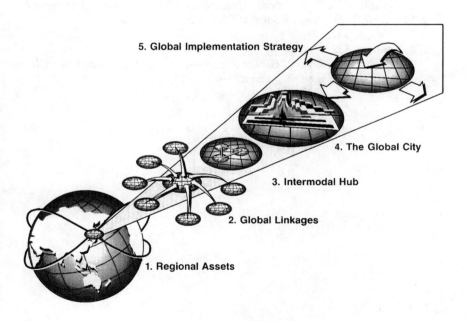

Figure 5.3. Linked infrastructure strategy.

ACKNOWLEDGMENTS

These remarks derive from the collective work and many years of experience of Bechtel's Regional Planning and Development Group on projects throughout the world. The author acknowledges and thanks the individual members of that group, both past and present, for their contributions to our current vision.

NOTES

1. Hoche-Mong, R. Stauffer, & K. Mpinga (a Bechtel study team). *Toward the Dynapolis*. San Francisco, CA: Bechtel Corporation.

2. Gilder, G. *Microcosm: The Quantum Revolution in Economics and Technology*. New York: Touchstone Books, 1989, p. 17.

3. Rothschild, M. *Bionomics—The Inevitability of Capitalism*. New York: Simon & Schuster, 1986.

4. Keegan, J. A. Wheatcraft. *Zones of Conflict: An Atlas of Future Wars*. New York: Holt and Rinehardt, 1986.

5. Larson, E., M. Ross, & R. Williams. "Beyond the Era of Materials," *Scientific American*, January 1986.

6. Naisbitt, J. & P. Aburdene. *Megatrends 2000—Ten New Directions for the 1990s*. New York: Avon Books, 1991, p. 329.

7. *Ibid.*, p. 332.

8. *Ibid.*, p. 332.

9. Knight, R. *Cities in a Global Society—Introduction: Redefining Cities*. Newbury Park, CA: Sage Publications, 1989, p. 15.

6

The Challenge to Smart Buildings: User-Controlled Ecological Environments for Productivity

Peter A. D. Mill
Volker Hartkopf
Vivian Loftness
Pleasantine Drake

WHAT IS A SMART OFFICE BUILDING?

Traditionally, building intelligence has been defined by the introduction of a long list of new products in telecommunications, electronics, security, automation, and building control systems. However, after ten years of use, this original definition has proven insufficient for ensuring the productive high-tech work environments anticipated by building owners and building occupants. A better definition would stipulate that building intelligence for the smart office provide unique and changing assemblies of recent technologies in appropriate physical, environmental, and organizational settings to enhance worker speed, understanding, communication, and overall productivity.[1] Three conditions must be achieved toward fulfilling the goal established in this definition.

First, the intelligent office building assembles or accommodates a flexible and adaptable package of recent technologies, resolving the full range of hardware for managing (1) external signal propagation; (2) external power; (3) telephone systems; (4) internal signal propagation; (5) computers—capacity, speed, and networking; (6) peripheral "inputters," processors, and "outputters"; (7) environmental controls and energy management; (8) security and fire safety systems; and (9) transport systems. The most comprehensive and continuously updated file of intelligent building products is compiled by the Intelligent Buildings in Washington D.C.

Second, the intelligent office building also ensures the appropriate physical and environmental settings for the range of hardware anticipated, thereby resolving the level of long-term flexibility or adaptability needed in (1) structure; (2) enclosure—walls, windows, roofs, and basement; (3) building geometry, from

53

Qualities needed for satisfactory total building performance

I.   Spatial Quality
    A. Workstation layout
    B. Workgroup layout
    C. Conveniences and services
    D. Amenities
    E. Occupancy factors and controls

II.   Thermal Quality
    A. Air temperature
    B. Mean radiant temperature
    C. Humidity
    D. Air speed
    E. Occupancy factors and controls

III. Air Quality
    A. Fresh air
    B. Fresh air distribution
    C. Restriction of mass pollution—gases, vapors, microorganisms, fumes, smokes, and dusts
    D. Restriction of energy pollution—ionizing radiation, microwaves, radio waves, light waves, and infrared light
    E. Occupancy factors and controls

IV.   Acoustic Quality
    A. Sound source—sound pressure levels and frequency
    B. Sound source—background noise
    C. Sound path—noise isolation (air and structureborne)
    D. Sound path—sound distribution, absorption, reflection, uniformity, and reverberation
    E. Occupancy factors and controls

V.   Visual Quality
    A. Ambient light levels—artificial and daylight
    B. Task light levels—artificial and daylight
    C. Contrast and brightness ratios
    D. Color rendition
    E. View, visual information
    F. Occupancy factors and controls

VI.   Building Integrity
    Based on knowledge of loads, moisture conditions, temperature shifts, air movement, radiation conditions, biological attack, and manmade and natural disasters
    A. Quality of mechanical/structural properties—compression, tension, shear, and abuse
    B. Quality of physical/chemical properties—watertightness, airtightness transmission, reflection, absorption of heat, light and sound energy, and fire safety
    C. Visible properties—color, texture, finish, form, durability, and maintainability

Figure 6.1. Responsibility of future office settings.

massing to orientation to horizontal and vertical plenum space to overall spatial organization; (4) major services such as power, heat, ventilation, air conditioning, lighting, and fire; and (5) interior elements such as ceiling, partitions, floor, and furniture systems. The 1985 ORBIT study was the first to identify the building responses necessary to accommodate intelligent building products (Davis et al., 1986).

Third, in the intelligent office building these physical components are not only evaluated independently in relation to the range of hardware to be accommodated in the building, but they are also evaluated in their integrated state to ensure that all critical environmental conditions are provided: (1) spatial quality, including physical safety and security; (2) thermal quality; (3) air quality; (4) acoustic quality; (5) visual quality; and (6) building integrity versus rapid degradation (Figure 6.1) (Hartkopf et al., 1986). The "high-tech" building must be evaluated for its suitability in accommodating the immediate electronic enhancements, as well as for its reliability and adaptability in accommodating future technologies and the anticipated level of long-term user requirements. Most recently, the National Academy of Sciences report on the Electronically Enhanced Office explored the relationship of intelligent building products and the physical and environmental responses needed.[2]

To achieve these three conditions (indeed, levels of innovation), the "intelligent" office building must reflect an unprecedented series of new steps in the buildings delivery process: (1) a long-term mission statement written with "expert" input anticipating the capacity for change; (2) clear goals for short- and long-term budgets; (3) a team decision-making process involving a range of experts with decision-making power from the project's outset (for cost-effectiveness and performance); (4) a performance design and construction contract with testable specifications; (5) a controlled building diagnostics process for quality assurance through design and construction; (6) an expert commissioning stage to lead into long-term expert maintenance and operation; and (7) a growing use field evaluation techniques and user questionnaires (POE) to assess the overall performance of the integrated system for building's occupancy.

Most critically, however, the intelligent office building clearly improves the quality of the workplace for the individual, representing a major philosophical change in office design. After all, what is the electronically enhanced office intended to facilitate, if not organizational effectiveness, worker speed, understanding, communication, productivity, and user health and well-being?

AN EVOLVING LIST OF MAJOR DESIGN CHANGES

The Advanced Building Systems Integration Consortium (ABSIC) at Carnegie Mellon University, Pittsburgh, has been involved in an effort to translate these critical conditions into an evolving list of building design and management changes needed in tomorrow's offices (Figure 6.2). Our three centers have been

AMP, Inc.
Harrisburg, Pennsylvania
Thomas Warne, Director, New Product Planing

Armstrong World Industries
Lancaster, Pennsylvania
Marshall Hemphill, Manager, Special Projects

Bechtel Corp.
Civil Company
San Francisco, California
Charles M. Spink, P. E., Manager,
Buildings and Infrastructure Operations
Coby Everdell, ATI, Manager of Technology
Carlos Pena, Manager of International Projects

Bell of Pennsylvania
Philadelphia, Pennsylvania
Ray Wickline, Director, Real Estate Engineering

Duquesne Light Company
Pittsburgh, Pennsylvania
William Bilka, Director, Marketing Development
Peggy Anne Page, Representative, Market Development

Johnson Controls
Milwaukee, Wisconsin
Ron Caffrey, Vice President, Marketing Systems and Services
Dennis Miller, Manager, Controls Research
Mike Demeter, Manager, Personal Environments Marketing

Manville Sales Corp.
Denver, Colorado
Jon F. Bauer, Senior Scientist
Robert Anderson, Vice President, Science and Technology

Producers Paint Group Industries
Pittsburgh, Pennsylvania
C. O. Peterson, Director of Marketing, Technical Services
Howard Thaller, Manager, Market Development Building Products

Westinghouse Electric
Pittsburgh, Pennsylvania
Charles Bell, Vice President, Central Region
Walter Mansfeld, Manager, Facilities Planning and Management
Richard Bell, Product Manager, Electronic Communications

Figure 6.2. List of active industry members of the Advanced Building Systems Integration Consortium.

relying on many years of Canadian government office assessments for total building performance using field diagnostic techniques and the ABSIC team was actively involved in the National Academy of Sciences' Building Research Board Committee on the Electronically Enhanced Office. From this committee's report, a list of major design changes that are occurring or must occur in the office of the future (Figure 6.3) acts as a basis for ABSIC's international field studies of intelligent buildings. This list, focusing on changes in the United States, has been consequently modified and developed at the Center for Building Performance and Diagnostics at Carnegie Mellon University, the Centres of Building Diagnostics at Ottawa and Dundee, with a consortium of building industries, to reflect recent developments and needs in intelligent offices in the United States, Japan, Germany, and the United Kingdom. Although the list of major design changes in the office of the future is evolving, some general findings in each country are described in the following sections. These international studies are a first step in the industry consortium's long-term effort to research, develop, and demonstrate office environments for innovations.

THE SMART, GREEN OFFICE ENVIRONMENT AND PRODUCTIVITY

Our ABSIC studies have shown that the modern office is growing into the United States' number one workplace, and understanding how to accommodate productive, clean environments in that context and in the global context have become critical. Attempts in the past decade to enhance productivity have taken a fragmented approach from the larger, open-office designs of the 1970s to centrally controlled energy management systems of the 1980s and more recently with information technology responding first with new electronic tools that although enhancing, are changing tasks and environmental needs of building occupants. The transition we are facing is not an easy one because the space and environmental controls existing in the 1970s and 1980s offices are not capable of easily accommodating the changes needed to establish improved productivity. Productivity in the workplace is dependent on factors including management, job satisfaction, income, status, context (state of economy), time spent in buildings, and interior environmental conditions. Studying office performance issues today shows that advancements in the past ten years have settled into three basic design approaches (Mill et al., 1987):

1. With state-of-the-art technology as controller (building intelligence or smart building), voice, data, and environmental information travel through one integrated path to a consolidated management system for security, fire, telephone, data management, environmental control (HVAC and light), and more.

1. Three-dimensional cable network (vertical and horizontal)
2. Multiple-zone HVAC network
3. Increased shared facilities
4. Improved lighting/daylighting control
5. Improved noise and pollution isolation
6. Redesigned workstations and workgroups, with alternative workplaces
7. Individualized environmental controls—light, heat, air, noise, and enclosure
8. Effective interior/envelope interface
9. More social settings, visual diversity
10. Building management trio with (CAFM)—facilities manager, technology manager, personnel manager

Questions

- Can the hardware cope with the proposed change?
- Can the physical/environment setting cope?
- Can the people and organizational structure cope?

Figure 6.3. Choices and decisions critical to the electronically enhanced office.

2. With the environment as controller (potentially labeled the decentralized building intelligence) repetitive local environmental sensors, controls, and event systems manage security, fire, data processing, and environmental needs. These environmental controllers can also provide energy management (thermostats to control unitary heat pumps, solar/temperature cells to control local sunshades, and daylight sensors to control perimeter lighting).
3. With the individual as controller (potentially labeled the user-intelligent building) local environmental sensors are often tied to central information processors, to inform occupants to manage and control security, fire, data, and environmental conditions (heat, cooling, air, and light) for energy effectiveness and comfort.

Over the past two decades, quality of working life has been an issue that has received considerable attention from governments to private-sector and professional organizations. This attention has concluded in results and professional opinion for the value of attaining the 1990s "the quality of working life" as a committed design goal, a committed maintenance objective, or a research focus. A Canadian Labour Congress (CLC) survey on the impact of VDUs on office working conditions in Canada emphasized that

Workplace stressors interact in combination with each other to produce more significant effects. Therefore when workplace improvements are proposed, the emphasis must be on a multi-factorial approach to maximize the positive benefits from such improvements. Workers needs must be a primary consideration in humanizing the workplace. (CLC, 1982; 63)

What has emerged as a critical perspective for the 1990s is that, whatever the links between job satisfaction and job performance, employee satisfaction with the physical environment is important to employee well-being, health, and productivity. Today quality of working life is seen as a specific "Green" program approach to addressing motivational issues by providing opportunities for challenge, responsibility, accomplishment, and pride through joint control and shared responsibility between employees and management. Finding alternative incentives is even more critical because many organizations predict fewer jobs in middle management in the future because of technological developments and fewer promotions. Incentives cited by Noe Palacios, Manager of Office Research for Steelcase, Inc. include pleasant work environment, job sharing, educational sabbaticals, and the redesign of some jobs to make them more interesting. Quality of working life has been defined as

a broad concept referring to work environment with minimal worker alienation and increased job satisfaction. Job satisfaction tends to be low when worker participation and autonomy are low and when work is comprised of fragmented and piecemeal tasks which allow workers little control over the final outcome of their work. Newer management work theories stress worker participation in decision-making and the humanization of the workplace through a variety of approaches, including worker participation, quality control circles, socio-technical systems, job enrichment, labor-management committees, and the ergonomic design of workspaces. (Dowall, 1986)

Ultimately, the introduction of new terminology and reorganization of task, whether they be facilities management or other office work processes, are insufficient. What is necessary is a significant shift of fundamental attitude toward individuals and groups of employees in the office. "For it is the facilities management department's attitude toward the employee, not the presence or absence of standards, that makes the difference between workplaces that foster productivity and those that foster frustration and discontent" (Prezzano, 1986).

Changing work patterns include flex-time, compressed work weeks, work done out of the building, and evening and overtime use of facilities. There is little economic justification in continuously lighting or conditioning empty or sporadically used space. The large, centrally controlled zones that typify smart office buildings built in the early 1980s are not responsive to these new needs. Under such conditions, conflicts emerge between demands to hold operating costs down and to provide reasonable work environments for employees as and when they work. Many authors discussing issues of environmental performance in buildings emphasize that a single set of environmental conditions will not provide comfort for all occupants (Hartkopf et al., 1985). Sundstrom (1986) defined this as the differential impact of the work environment depending on characteristics of the person, the job, the group, and the organization. Many authors recommend that some adjustments for local conditions be given to individuals. Similarly, other authors cite that people are more likely to be annoyed by an environmental condition, such as noise, that is not within their control (Michael & Bienvenue, 1983).

USER INTEGRATION: A NEEDED CONTROL
FOR THE SMART OFFICE

Systems integration for local control is not a future fantasy as was shown in 1892–85 with Public Works Canada FUNDI/DOC field trials (Mill et al., 1986). As electronic enhancement of buildings with respect to centralized management systems for security, fire, telephone, data processing, energy management, and environmental controls evolves, there are distinct alternative design approaches. These approaches have different loci of control, ranging from technology as controller in the intelligent building or the environment as a decentralized locus of control to individual users, with local environmental sensors and central information processors providing information to occupants.

The present smart building approach basically represents a technologically centered idea, not a human centered one, extending the notion that building occupants detrimentally affect environmental performance. However, current central energy control systems (ECMS) already fail to perform as envisioned, without the added complexity of data and telecommunications management . . . Moreover, current centrally managed environmental control systems have not demonstrated capability in coping with major changes in building functions, rapid changes in activities, or rapid changes in exterior environmental conditions. Instead they demonstrate unacceptable sluggishness in the face of dynamic environments. (Loftness et al., 1986, 339)

OFFICE VAGRANCY; A HIDDEN DEBT IN
THE PRODUCTIVE 1990s

A priority to establish an approach for smart offices must respond to issues of health, well-being, productivity-cost-benefit, and user environmental control. This is evident when examining the performance of offices built during the 1970s and 1980s, especially when one relates the total building performance of any building during its forty-year life cycle. Occupancy salaries and the building operation and capital costs show that capital costs incurred to provide a building are 2 percent of a forty-year life-cycle cost, and operation and maintenance incur another 6 percent to 8 percent of the total costs. The remaining forty-year expenditure, 92 percent of the cost, is in salaries.

These major costs can be annually distributed as salaries at $200 to $400.00 per square foot per year, whereas energy equates out at only $.80 to $1.50 per square foot per year and maintenance is $.50 to $2.00 per square foot per year with the property costs between $4.00 to $20.00 per square foot per year. Data derived from other building studies by Public Works Canada showed that 25 percent of the occupants are often absent from their desks 25 percent of the time. This occupant absenteeism was found to be attributable to different accumulations of stressful environmental conditions ranging from visual quality through to the poor air quality. Yet these buildings all met the indoor environmental standards of their time to which the building's intelligence was responding correctly. If this vagrancy persists, then employee absenteeism will eventually occur.

The staggering consequence of this absenteeism is shown in the following example. If we consider a 120,000-square-foot building in which there are 800 persons who on average earn $15,000 then the payroll is more than $10 million per year. Consequently, if 1 percent in absenteeism occurs because of poor management of the office ecology, then $100,000 per year is lost. This acute symptom does not consider further losses caused by the cyclical daily practice of workstation vagrancy caused by chronic headaches from either eye strain, hot temperature, or stuffiness. Consequently, the total loss to the employer in productive hours incurred through illness or workstation vagrancy equates within several years to a loss comparable to the actual building cost of a smart building.

THE SMART OFFICE IN THE UNITED STATES: A FOCUS ON THE WORKSTATION AND PRODUCTIVITY

The greatest development in U.S. advanced office settings centers around the workstation. Each individual workstation now includes a vast range of electronic peripherals (telephones, mini- or microcomputers, printers, and FAX machines), housed in newer ergonomic and computer-capable furnishing systems, and supported by cable management floor systems and, for the first time in modern offices, individual environmental control systems—a response to the growing need for passive environments in striving for the smarter office.

Major building design changes consistently include the introduction of a three-dimensional cable network at the top of the list, involving both vertical and horizontal cable distribution plenums. U.S. manufacturers and designers have developed a range of solutions for horizontal distribution from overhead cable trays to poke through trench systems, and raised floors below (access floors that are structurally and acoustically sound). However, further development is needed in flexible and expandable horizontal cable management technologies and their effective connection with the worksurface. In addition, buildingwide vertical distribution has been unsatisfactorily considered in the early design stages, with inadequate vertical chase space inappropriately located and accessed.

Second, there has been a shift toward multiple-zone HVAC systems, a move away from four- or five-zone VAV controls to local fan coils and dual-duct systems or at least multiple VAV controls that offer more local variation in temperature delivery. Recently, following the development of the multiple-zone HVAC, there has been renewed development in individual environmental control technologies for personally setting light, heat, fresh air, and air conditioning levels (Woods, 1982).

The most significant product development in this area is the personal environments (PEM) by Johnson Controls, in which fresh air is ducted to each desk in an open office environment, with dimmer controls for cool air, radiant heat, task light, and even white noise. Personal controls can effectively resolve individual sensitivities to common building inadequacies (Figure 6.4). The ABSIC studies of the personal environmental approach have found that it effectively addresses the contemporary ecological and productivity problem in smart offices. Its design provides for lower operating costs (5 percent to 8 percent), lower building first costs (10 percent), while providing an unprecedented user control over a broader range of personal environmental needs. The reduction in energy computes out to at least 5 percent. However, this turns out to be insignificant when compared to the increase in user well-being(at least 1 percent reduction in absenteeism) and productivity issues (at least 2 percent).

Please indicate the extent to which you agree or disagree with each of the statements about this building overall: "This building is healthy to be in."

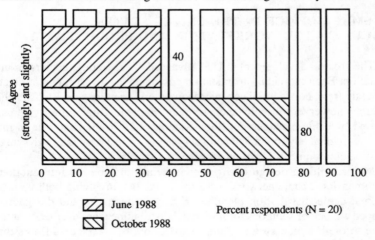

Figure 6.4. Effectiveness of personal control in resolving individual sensitivities to common building inadequacies.

In addition to these ecological and productivity challenges for tomorrow's smart building, the American office is beginning to show the effects of increased computer memory capability, with mainframe rooms being replaced by mini-VAXes and microprocessors at every workstation, linked through local area networks. The shift away from mainframes and dummy terminals does not diminish the number of shared facilities, however; group spaces for printers, FAX machines, copiers, electronic conferencing, social spaces, and kitchens are growing.

To end the list, there have been a few examples of a shift in the design process toward team decision-making to ensure the creation of a truly intelligent office. Most notable is the TRW headquarters project in Cleveland, where a full-time project manager coordinated a team of equal decision-makers, including an exterior architect, an interior architect, a mechanical engineer, a telecommunications engineer, and a building constructor. This design team was fully involved from early conceptual design through one year of commissioning to ensure an office headquarters with the latest in technology and the physical and environmental setting needed to support the technology over time.

THE SMART OFFICE IN JAPAN: A FOCUS ON THE CORE

When looking at Japanese intelligent office buildings (including Toshiba's Headquarters, Ark Hills, and Takenaka's Umeda Center) it is clear that the emphases are on the advanced design of the building core and its servicing systems rather than on workstations or on building enclosures. Although the list of major intelligent design changes includes a rethinking of the 3-D cable network (as in the United States), the vertical distribution is far better resolved through distributed cores than the horizontal. The assumption appears to be that the workstation arrangement will remain static, while the workstation hardware will change. Multiple-zone HVAC has also been embraced in the Japanese office but with distributed mechanical systems rather than space-by-space mixing devices. These distributed mechanical rooms vary from one every three floors to four per floor, providing for more thermal variation and control in the constantly changing office setting.

On the other hand, there is far more development in Japan of technologies for resource conservation (energy, water, and air), including gray water management, thermoelectric cooling, load balancing, and off-peak storage. There is also more far-reaching development of systems for fire and earthquake management, and systems for vertical transportation (elevator and "communication" fire stairs), all located in the well-developed core. Most unprecedented is the development in postoccupancy robotics for continuous environmental testing (temperature, air quality, and noise done at Ark Hill) and for unmanned window washing.

Japan is also a leader in team decision-making. The design process encourages team decision strategies from the outset from architects, engineers, constructors, and facilities managers. The missing link, however, is the organized introduction of occupant input into workstation design and servicing and into individual environmental requirements for light, heat, air, and sound control.

THE SMART OFFICE IN GERMANY:
A FOCUS ON THE RESPONSIVE ENCLOSURE

Although polar differences were not sought by the ABSIC team in their international studies, the German intelligent office designs (including Colonia Insurance Headquarters, Daimler Benz Headquarters, Nixdorf Regional Offices, and the Institute for Applied Microelectronics) focused more on the building shell than on either the core emphasized in Japan, or the workstation emphasized in the United States. Many "intelligent" office buildings in Germany are shifting toward six- or seven-story buildings rather than high rises, with greatly increased exposure to the landscape through campus planning, green atria for social spaces and circulation, and smaller floor plates.

Daylight and artificial light interfaces have been explored, and management systems have been developed, including exterior sunshading devices and distributed lighting controls. Siemens is developing window lenses to evenly distribute daylight for working light levels deep into office bays and to eliminate glare. Air flow windows and water-heated framing technologies use waste heat from the highly automated office to minimize occupant discomfort, energy loads, and building degradation. The interface of mechanical ventilation and operable windows for fresh air is also explored, with climate sensors to inform the central system and the occupant. The concern about unhealthy building products is growing with rising interest in all natural products and finishes.

This emphasis on environmental interface has led to a broad range of intelligent office technologies including distributed lighting systems on movable tethers in the ceiling and distributed air systems on movable tethers in the floor. The movable air supply ports are fed by central systems with distributed controls or by individual heat pumps. This interest in individual air supply has led to the simultaneous development of raised-floor technologies for air and cable management. Early raised floors were acoustic failures (because of vibration, footfall, and squeak sounds), but new technologies are evolving, including the Schmidt-Reuter "eggcrate" floor system, to provide structural soundness and adequate air and cable management space.

Although there is some emphasis on introducing new cabling technologies, new computer technologies, and new desktop peripherals, the German intelligent office focuses more on providing the vertical and horizontal plenums and on the environmental systems needed for the introduction of future computer hardware than on the rapid development of that hardware. Indeed, the intelligent office concept has led to a largely different industry growth in quiet individual heat pumps, lighting and shading systems, and accessible and easily modifiable central mechanical and electrical frameworks.

In contrast to Japan and the United States, the German building delivery process consistently involves the ultimate users of the building from the project outset. It is these long-hour, long-term building users who have launched the German intelligent office into the "fresh air architecture" directions that are pursued today. As a result, a high-quality work environment for each occupant is pursued, with more individual or small group offices, to maximize access to daylight, fresh air, and landscaped gardens and courts.

THE SMART OFFICE IN THE UNITED KINGDOM: A FOCUS ON MATERIAL AND DETAIL FOR AESTHETICS AND PERFORMANCE QUALITIES

The office buildings of United Distillers, the Grinian, and the Lloyds of London that were studied by the ABSIC team revealed a fascination with materials and detail for their aesthetic qualities, justified through potential higher performance qualities. All three buildings used a limited set of high-integrity materials—lead, stone, stainless steel, glass, and natural wood—to create an enduring modern aesthetic. Each material led to the development of critical detailing, with the support of industry, to ensure immediate high-performance quality and long-term integrity. A restricted number of materials and corresponding details were chosen to ensure an equal level of resolution and appropriate integration decision-making. In addition, the architects sought an increased exposure of these select materials and details through highly articulated building forms and interior cutouts (courts and atria) that increased overall surface finish, and daylight exposure.

More significant, however, is the engineering expressionism that developed in the Lloyds of London building, designed to ensure accessibility and expandability given major changes in technology. The exposed service cores, with each subsystem (mechanical supply and return, electrical, telecommunication, and transportation) independently run on the exterior of the building, create the building aesthetic and its long-term flexibility. These accessible exterior "cores" are a reminder of the large accessible interior cores in Japan and Germany, although these are far more expressive and expandable.

Interior design also demonstrated the use of a limited number of high-quality materials and well-resolved details, with performance as a justification. Highly engineered light and ceiling fixtures were generated from a desire to provide glareless light and individual control (in heavily automated workplaces) and to provide effective acoustic absorption with modest reflection and effective return air (in very high-density workplaces). The engineering of the air flow windows in Lloyds of London was also displayed as an aesthetic both inside and out, with supply and return ducts exposed outside of each unit.

Finally, there is a significant cultural and political tradition in the United Kingdom in the form of "right-to light" laws that continues to positively affect the design of modern high-tech buildings. No workstations are designed without direct visual access to windows, building depths are controlled, and courts and atria are designed to maximize sunlight penetration (sunlight "cones"). Clear glass with overhangs continue to be the norm. Daylight has been used traditionally in the United Kingdom as the primary source of working light in shallow plan buildings. The two-story Grinian building in the speculative Dundee High Technology Park effectively provides working daylight for deeper open office areas through the use of clear glass sloped inward to the sill and a corresponding upwardly sloped ceiling. There is also a continuing interest in the United Kingdom in passive solar designs for heating, cooling, and lighting of commercial buildings. Although there is some speculation that the United Kingdom will go through a period of sealed air-conditioned buildings and reflective glass because of the global warming trends and the greatly increased internal gains, this trend is already being negated by building research groups and by office workers currently benefiting from access to windows, clear views, and sunshine.

One can argue that the system "aesthetics" found in the United Kingdom took over in the design process at one point, leaving the component's independent or integrated performance behind. Nonetheless, there are major lessons to be learned from the careful and limited selection of materials (including daylight), as well as the careful resolution of details and integrations (with the support of industry), toward creating a durable and flexible building for increasing and everchanging automation.

CONCLUSION

The Advanced Building Systems Integration Consortium based at Carnegie Mellon University and in conjunction with our other two centers in Canada and Scotland is convinced that advanced building environments, or smart offices, must be fundamentally designed for "greener performance standards" for appropriate spatial, thermal, visual, acoustic and air quality, as well as long-term integrity. The declining interest in only intelligent buildings, described in the Steelcase Office Environment Index 89 (Figure 6.5), is in fact a declining interest in an overly automated assembly of hardware and not a declining interest in intelligent ecological environments, indicated in the many other high-priority factors.

The creation of appropriate settings for current and future office technologies and activities depends on a better process and a more flexible, occupant-sensitive product (Hartkopf et al., 1985). Questions of closed versus open offices, of 3-D cable management, of central versus distributed mechanical systems, of movable lights and air supply, of individual occupant control, and of carefully selected materials and equipment at the workstation, must be explored. In new buildings intended to provide the optimum "environment for innovation," the question must not be of which current technologies should be tightly woven together but of what settings should be created to handle today's, and tomorrow's, technologies. Most provocatively, the question of indoor fresh air architecture must be explored,

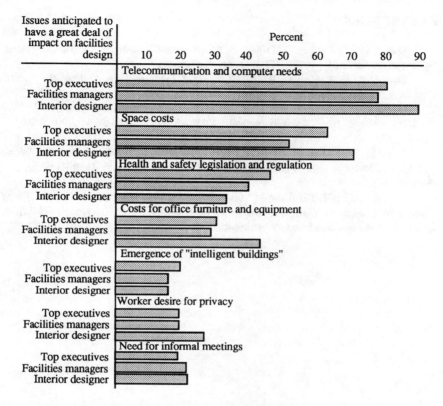

Figure 6.5. Steelcase, IBD, IFMA office environment index.

reconnecting the gold-collar worker with natural products, daylight, natural ventilation, or ventilation from regenerative filtered processes and access to the outdoors.

NOTES

1. Advanced Building Systems Integration Consortium, Center for Building Performance and Diagnostics, Carnegie Mellon University: Studies of Advanced Technology and Intelligent Buildings, 1988.

2. Electronically Enhanced Office Buildings, National Academy of Sciences, Building Research Board, National Research Council, 1988.

REFERENCES

Davis, G., F. Becker, F. Duffy, & W. Simms. *Organizations, Buildings and Information Technology,* ORBIT-2 Overview Report. 1986.

Drake, P. & A. Kaplan. *DOC/OCS Field Trial of Environmental Studies.* Ottawa, Canada: Department of Communications, 1988.

Hartkopf, V., V. Loftness, & P. Mill. "Integration for Performance." In *The Building Systems Integration Handbook,* R. Rush (ed.). New York: John Wiley & Sons, 1985.

Mill, P., V. Loftness, & V. Hartkopf. "Evaluating the Quality of the Work Place." In *The Ergonomic Payoff,* edited by R. Leuder. Toronto: Holt Rinehart and Wilson, 1986.

Woods, J. E. "Do Buildings Make You Sick?" In *Proceedings of the Third Canadian Buildings Congress on Achievements and Challenges in Building.* Ottawa, Canada: Canadian Government, 1982.

7

Multifunction Polis:
Partnering for a Global Technopolis

James Hudak

The multifunction polis (MFP) is an inelegant name for an elegant concept: two countries, Australia and Japan, acting jointly and purposively to create a city of the future. This MFP was conceived to better demonstrate possible urban forms and life-styles and to foster a commercial and institutional framework supportive of the emerging growth industries of the twenty-first century.

This chapter describes the evolution of the MFP concept. It begins by describing the positions of the Japanese and Australian participants and then describes the unified concept that emerged in the first six months of the MFP feasibility study to reconcile the initial positions. This unified concept was tested during interviews with sixty-two senior executives from international corporations and educational institutions in Europe, Asia, and the Americas. These executives were seen as a test market for potential investors. The concluding sections of the chapter describe the results of this test marketing work and the resulting final concept of the MFP.

THE JAPANESE POSITION

The MFP was first proposed at the Japan-Australia Ministerial Committee Meeting in January 1987 by the Japanese Minister for International Trade and Industry (MITI) to the Australian Minister for Industry, Technology and Commerce. This was followed in September 1987 by the release of a paper prepared by MITI, *A Multifunction Polis Scheme for the 21st Century*—otherwise known as the *Basic Concept Paper*—which outlined the Japanese perspective.

The *Basic Concept Paper* identified four fundamental trends critical to social and economic development in the next century:

1. The internationalization of business and economies
2. The increasing rate of technical innovation
3. The fundamental importance of information flows and information technology for all forms of economic activity
4. The aging of societies in industrialized nations.

The *Basic Concept Paper* argued that each trend has consequences for how people live. For example, growing international exchange implies the need for systems of education that foster a cosmopolitan outlook. Similarly, technological innovation offers the possibility of widening the scope of choice for human activity. The aging of society and its corollary of a longer productive working life creates new needs for adult and recurrent education to keep pace with technological change and to provide new opportunities for personal satisfaction.

Together, these trends and the changing life-styles they imply pose a formidable challenge to urban life as currently constituted. The *Basic Concept Paper* proposed a joint Japanese-Australian endeavor to meet this challenge. The basis of this international cooperation was the nations' position as industrialized countries in a fast-developing region. In addition, Australia's attempts to reposition itself in the global economy and Japan's interest in internationalization offered possibilities for mutual benefit.

The city of the future vision expressed in the *Basic Concept Paper* is based on a critique of contemporary urban life. In this view, cities are instruments through which humanity has aspired to create an integrated, satisfying environment. However, the recent history of urban life can be described as a process of progressive disintegration in which "the various sophisticated functions. . . have really materialized as a mere aggregate of separate functions rather than as an urban organic whole" (*Basic Concept Paper*, 1987). This disintegration is expressed in a series of stages, or spheres, each corresponding roughly to historical periods (Table 7.1).

The *Basic Concept Paper* stated that a reintegration of the elements of urban life, work, home, education, and recreation is both desirable and necessary in a twenty-first-century city. The possibility of such a utopian city, a city of the Fifth Sphere, is the visionary idea that motivated the Japanese proposal.

Just as the Fifth Sphere life-style integrates home and office, recreation and leisure, and education and work, so the economy of a Fifth Sphere city combines high-tech and high-touch industries. In this conception, the MFP acts as an incubator of twenty-first-century industries by linking enterprises based on advanced technology with a life-style and an urban framework that supports human creativity. To this mix would be added a cosmopolitan component through extended visits for study or research by overseas scientists, artists, entrepreneurs, and other professionals. These professionals would be drawn to the MFP's extensive system of recurrent and advanced education.

Table 7.1. The Five Spheres of Historical Development of the City

Sphere	Function	Era
First	Home and workplace combined.	Medieval
Second	Home and workplace divided.	Industrial Revolution
Third	Recreation emerged as an independent realm distinct from the first two spheres.	Early twentieth century
Fourth	A transfer of the third sphere in time and location and an extension of conventional life-style. Combined with the diversification of life-style and values, the need for resorts for extended stays is rapidly growing.	Late twentieth century
Fifth	A combination of all the elements of the four spheres but in a city not classifiable under any one of them. The realization of a MFP.	Twenty-first century

The *Basic Concept Paper* identified two essential criteria for commercial development in the MFP: the MFP must provide opportunities for investment by Japanese businesses, and these investments should build on Australia's existing strengths. These strengths include political stability, high standards of education, skilled labor, a sophisticated infrastructure, abundant natural resources, and a high level of scientific and technical accomplishment. Using these criteria, the *Basic Concept Paper* identified three high-tech industries and two high-touch industries with potential for the MFP:

- *The High-Tech Industries.* Biotechnology, new materials, and computer software are considered fast growing and fundamental to economic life in the next century.
- *The High-Touch Industries.* Convention services and the resort industry are considered consistent with Australia's strengths and with the vision and theme for the MFP.

In addition to commercial opportunities in high-tech and high-touch industries, the *Basic Concept Paper* also identified several areas as essential to the development of the MFP: health care, education, information systems, and transportation. For each area, innovative systems were suggested to help realize the "organic integration of functions" implicit in the Fifth Sphere concept and to act as magnets for investment in the MFP. Together, these new systems constitute a "soft" or "software" infrastructure that will be as essential to city life in the next century as the pipes, tunnels, roads, and wires of the traditional "hard" infrastructure are to contemporary cities.

The *Basic Concept Paper* described the MFP as a semiresidential city rather than as a center of conventional residential life. The MFP is envisaged as a commuter destination to which people come for several weeks to several years before returning to their home base. Although the *Basic Concept Paper* was not explicit about the participants in the MFP community, its emphasis on research, development, resorts, and conventions suggested a community of professionals positioned to take advantage of the educational and other amenities of life in the MFP. These people will generally be in the prime of their working lives, although older and retired people may also take advantage of the possibilities for adult education. Except as family members of the visiting professionals, young people do not figure strongly in the MFP concept as expressed in the *Basic Concept Paper*. The *Basic Concept Paper* was also largely silent on how many people might live in the MFP; however, its analysis of transportation systems for the development suggested a minimum scale of 50,000-100,000 inhabitants.

The sophisticated functions assumed for the MFP typically require a large urban setting or megalopolis. However, the *Basic Concept Paper* criticized the lack of humanity and the limited opportunities for mutual exchange and contact offered by existing urban centers. Instead, a new city was imagined that would be constituted on more human dimensions. Such a city would possess the following spatial attributes:

- The ability to achieve urban integration so that human scale and interaction can be achieved. This would relate to particular site characteristics such as topography and landform. Walking distances between home, work and recreation must be kept to an acceptable level
- An attractive climate to encourage a range of outdoor recreation, leisure, and cultural pursuits
- A physically beautiful location and a unique design to attract international visitors
- Accessibility to an international airport
- Relatively simple site characteristics to minimize construction and acquisition costs.

In summary, these characteristics point to a remote but accessible greenfield site in a beautiful location.

THE AUSTRALIAN POSITION

In contrast to the Japanese *Basic Concept Paper,* the Australian perspective was rooted in the more immediate concerns of domestic economic development. The MFP initiative was welcomed as an opportunity to assist Australia in achieving its full potential in both the Asia-Pacific and the global economies.

However, the Australian perspective also reflected a concern that the MFP might be realized in ways not consistent with the objectives of economic development. The Australian response was governed by nine principles that established the ground rules for Australia's participation in the MFP (Figure 7.1).

Much of the work of elaborating the Australian perspective on the MFP was carried out by MFP Australia Research (MFPAR), the Australian Domestic Committee. In the Australian analysis, four key trends determined the shape of domestic wealth-creating activity:

1. The internationalization of business and Australia's increasing reliance on international trade
2. The rapid growth of Asia and the Pacific as an economic region
3. A growing emphasis on value-added manufacturing and services rather than on commodity production
4. A resultant need to strengthen links between research and development activities and downstream activities.

The MFP is seen as providing a platform for wealth creation through internationalization of those sectors of the Australian economy that have the potential to be highly successful in the Asia and the Pacific and the global market. In addition, the MFP is seen as playing a catalytic role in promoting structural change in the Australian economy. The MFP could play this role by attracting a critical mass of expertise, providing a test bed function for new products and services, or developing an innovative soft infrastructure. Wealth creation through economic restructuring, combined with appropriate redistribution mechanisms, will benefit all Australians. The vision of increased wealth for all Australians was the driving force behind the Australian conception of the MFP.

The concentration on economic development leads to a fundamentally different thematic Australian focus than that postulated in the Japanese *Basic Concept Paper*. For the Japanese, the MFP is a place in which certain desirable activities could take place. In the Australian view, the MFP is a set of desirable activities that may be bound spatially, depending on the requirements of the activities. The link between the activities might be physical, as in a high-speed train connection between R&D centers, or the link might be virtual, as with a sophisticated communications and information network. Whatever the nature of the linkages between activities, they would all share a common identity as MFP activities. This identity, with its overtones of leading-edge technology and world-class competitiveness, would function as an international brand name distinguishing the activities of the MFP and acting as a drawing card to international investors.

1. The development of an MFP based on internationally traded information, education and training, leisure and tourism, and research and development activities should be in Australia's interest, with particular emphasis on the pursuit of scientific and technological excellence. The MFP should be developed to assist structural change in the Australian economy geared toward the development of an internationally competitive and export-oriented industry structure.

2. Fundamental to the competitive advantage of the concept is the development of leading-edge infrastructures in telecommunications, information, and education.

3. The MFP should be truly international in its links with the work economy, its investment sources, and its participants.

4. The MFP should be developed as an entity that is not an enclave but is linked with the remainder of the Australian economy, providing a leading-edge test bed and encouraging technology transfer.

5. Further work should be undertaken on the assumption that the proposal will proceed to fruition only if it can mobilize significant private-investor support, particularly in Japan and other countries, which results in a net addition to available capital resources in Australia.

6. The MFP should not be financed through the provision of special location-specific commonwealth and state subsidies.

7. The feasibility study should investigate a range of urban development options, including those involving multiple sites, all of which assume that the MFP not be a cultural enclave but rather be integrated with Australian society.

8. The commonwealth government should have carriage of all negotiations with the Japanese government for the implementation of the MFP principles. The states may discuss commercial proposals and provide information to the Japanese government.

9. The commonwealth and state governments are committed to examining the regulatory environment to facilitate investment in the MFP. In particular, the commonwealth government will examine the climate for the movement of people, money, and goods in a positive way to enhance the MFP proposal.

Figure 7.1. Australia's nine principles of the MFP.

The MFPAR explored a wide range of commercial opportunities in value-added services and value-added manufacturing in nearly twenty industry areas. The commercial opportunities explored broadly overlap those listed in the *Basic Concept Paper*. In addition, areas regarded as part of the soft infrastructure in the *Basic Concept Paper* were explored as areas of potential commercial opportunity in the

MFPAR analysis. Although the Australian work was explicitly commercial in its focus, its emphasis on economic restructuring requires that the MFP must be fully integrated with existing Australian urban functions. The Australian perspective also suggests the need for an information technology-based soft infrastructure to keep Australian cities competitive in the next century.

The Australian perspective on MFP inhabitants began with considerations of the role of the MFP as an agent for change in the national economy. This suggests that all Australians are potential users of the activities associated with the MFP, as employers or employees, consumers, or even tourists. This idea of the MFP being used by all Australians was underscored in the injunction, contained in the Australian nine principles, that the MFP shall not be an economic or cultural enclave.

The Australian perspective is not explicit about the spatial form that the MFP may take. However, an analysis of the Australian position reveals the following, implicit, formal attributes:

- Development from an existing infrastructure base
- A critical mass of activities
- A variety of industrial activity
- Ready access
- A marketable location with an existing cultural and economic base
- Cultural diversity.

Spatial analysis conducted in the site-ranking phase of the consultancy concluded that locations which are efficient for private-sector-led development and which will foster cultural diversity are more likely to be found within major metropolitan areas. The scale of Australian geography, the spatial distribution of the population within it and the political imperatives arising therefrom also imply an MFP at more than one location.

THE UNIFIED CONCEPT

On April 10, 1989, the Joint Steering Committee adopted a unified concept for the MFP. This concept was a framework in which both the Japanese and the Australian perspectives might be accommodated. This unified concept, augmented by subsequent industry and spatial analysis, was the foundation for the test-marketing phase of the feasibility study.

The search for integration—for harmony—in city life expressed in the Japanese concept and the focus on economic activity in the Australian perspective find common ground in the idea of economic sustainability. A pleasing and prosperous urban area must also reconcile itself to the needs of the environment. This presents a fundamental challenge to existing notions of urban design and of urban commerce. The possibility of a future-oriented development dedicated to technical advancement and economic growth in harmony with the environment is the vision that underlies the unified concept (Figure 7.2).

Each component of the vision—humanity, technology, and the environment—corresponds to differing city functions and economic activities. These functions and activities are grouped under the labels of renaissance city, technopolis, and biosphere. For example, the renaissance city features industries relating to human potential such as health services, tourism, resort and convention services, and education. Similarly, the renaissance city corresponds to urban design challenges such as the need to maximize opportunities for face-to-face interaction. Grouped in this way, the theme expressed in the unified concept is adaptable to multiple functions at multiple sites or to multiple functions in a single site.

Twelve target industries were studied for inclusion in the unified concept. Of the twelve, five were selected as particular priorities for test marketing. These were education, health, information technology/telecommunications, leisure and media, and environment. Transportation, construction and design, and agriculture were considered to have potential for the MFP but were given a lower priority for test marketing. For each priority industry, a commercial focus was developed consistent with industry trends and the complimentary strengths of Australia and Japan. In addition, a soft infrastructure of "seed institutions" was proposed. These new institutions would stimulate activity that would otherwise not take place.

Like the Japanese concept, the unified MFP concept envisions an international community of researchers, designers, and other professionals and their families. Many of these people would be visitors staying for a limited time. However, this small community of roughly 20,000 inhabitants would be thoroughly connected, even immersed, in the larger Australian environment. The hope is to strike a tension-balance in which the MFP retains a sense of community while being fully integrated with the surrounding areas.

The unified MFP concept describes the spatial configuration of the MFP as a single site in a major metropolitan area or a limited number of sites in a number of metropolitan areas. Small specialist nodes linked with the major center or centers are also considered possible. Here too, the concept combines aspects of the Japanese perspective—the MFP as a place—with elements of the Australian perspective—the MFP in existing metropolitan areas.

The site design qualities include

- A critical mass of economic activity balanced by a sense of community and place
- A diversity of settings in the site or sites
- Architecture that facilitates face-to-face interaction and is distinctive enough to function as an international symbol for the MFP
- Urban areas accessible by foot
- Extensive and innovative use of public space.

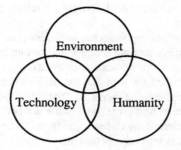

Figure 7.2. The unified MFP concept.

INPUT FROM WORLDWIDE TEST MARKETING

Worldwide test marketing further refined the MFP concept. Investors found the notion of deliberately creating a city of the future appealing. Investors also stipulated that they wish to see the MFP become a truly international place. MFP's environment, humanity, and technology themes have a clear marketing appeal. However, these themes need to be seen for what they are—"handles" that enable the overall MFP concept to be quickly grasped rather than themselves being areas of extensive commercial opportunity.

The test-marketing outcomes also suggested a narrower, better-defined set of functions. The areas that appear to be most promising relate to education, health care, telecommunications, and media production and broadcasting. International investor responses suggest that in those areas Australia has an opportunity to build international centers of excellence and establish regionally oriented resource pools. There is also significant interest, although more regionally specialized, in resort-based activities and commercial opportunities in environmental management.

In terms of institutional activities, it is clear that the MFP must have a focus on education at its core. All institutional activities that received international investor endorsement have education at their center:

- An international teaching and research institute specializing in environmental sciences and telecommunications
- A world-class health care teaching facility
- Corporate training, conference, and teleconference facilities
- Language translation institutes to support regional media production and broadcasting.

International investors endorsed the idea that the MFP site should be within an existing metropolitan envelope. They saw it as essential that the MFP be collocated in this way to ensure access to much-valued amenities derived from major metropolises. These include access to international airports, universities and research institutes, the cultural and life-style offerings of major cities, and the opportunities for ethnic mix.

While advocating a "metropolitan brownfields" size, investors recognized the need for the MFP to achieve its own identity and not be invisibly embedded in an overall metropolitan fabric. Importantly, international respondents to the test-marketing program dismissed the idea that the MFP could succeed if it were small scale. Instead, they stressed the need for the MFP to achieve regional and international visibility and to be a "real" city. Scale is a particularly difficult attribute to measure because it means many different things to different people. So far as it is possible to generalize, it is unlikely that a place of much less than 200,000 people would be seen as having sufficient scale to warrant significant international investor participation.

International investors also rejected ideas that the MFP could have multiple or networked sites. They stressed the need to focus, at least initially, on a single and major MFP location for international investment. This single site is seen by investors as needing to have physical characteristics consistent with the city of the future vision and with the environment theme.

CONCLUSION

The MFP concept is a city of the future in Australia developed through international collaboration and that meets the environmental, life-style, and technological challenges of city life in the next century. The MFP will have a diverse economic base of knowledge-intensive industries built around a core of education. The MFP will act as a magnet for international knowledge workers and investors while offering opportunities to a cross-section of Australian society. The form of the MFP will enhance human vitality, be responsive to change, and be an intelligent environment.

Much progress has been made in the three years since the MFP was first proposed. The governments of Japan and Australia must make decisions on site and other future steps to turn the concept into reality, and the road to reality will not be easy. Our ability to define the technical and economic processes necessary to form a technopolis have far exceeded our ability to define the social processes necessary for acceptance. The MFP became a major issue during the Australian national election in March 1990. Strong opposition to the MFP formed on issues from racism and opposition to Japanese investment in the Australian economy to legitimate questions about the role and benefit in the Australian economy of a city of the future. The Labor Party retained power, although by a narrow margin, and Senator Button has since declared the MFP a "goer." Much remains to be done to achieve the vision, but the MFP stands as one of the world's most exciting examples of international partnering and a concept that will stimulate others to think about the technopolis.

NOTES

1. This chapter is extracted from the *Consultancy Final Report* for the Multifunction Polis Feasibility Study presented to the MFP Joint Secretariat in December 1989 by Andersen Consulting/Kinhill. The author of this chapter was the project director for the consultancy.

8

Future Sites for High-Technology Development in the Former Soviet Union

Viacheslav Pis'menny

Consideration is given to development trends of Soviet "science towns" built during the past several decades. The Moscow suburb city of Troitsk, center of research in general and nuclear physics, is an example of the necessity of reconstructing the infrastructure of Soviet research centers. Complementing the existing potential of large institutes with infrastructure accommodated to the needs of small research and production companies, liquidation of disproportions in the social infrastructure, and openness to international partnership are factors that should create a healthy environment for efficient scientific work in the former Soviet Union.

Recent changes in the former Soviet Union have affected all social structures of the country. In particular, these changes directly refer to science and its social niche. Questions are raised: Why, while keeping one of the leading positions in the world in the number of scientists and engineers, does the former Soviet Union noticeably lag behind many Western countries in technology? Why is the Soviet industry so imperceptive to new ideas, repelling them and dooming science to fruitlessness? Why is science satisfied with its role of idea generator and not interested in implementing new ideas into industry by properly commercializing them?

Of course, radical solutions are seen on the route of social transformations. However, analysis of the current situation reserves a significant place for the operation and efficiency of the "research–production" link.

Let's consider the common trends with the example of a southern Moscow suburb with its center in Troitsk. This small town (population about 30,000), located by a major highway and surrounded with picturesque woods, is a home for seven institutes (mostly with physics profiles) of the USSR Academy of Sciences and the well-known Kurchatov Atomic Energy Institute. More than 10,000 Troitsk citizens are employees of these institutes. Other citizens provide the necessary support for research and growth, build houses and offices in town, teach children in schools and preschools, work in clinics, and maintain stores. During the past ten to fifteen years, the institutes and the town itself have been growing at about 10 percent to 15 percent annually, and today's rate is the same. It has been calculated that the town will double in size in fifteen years.

Troitsk is a typical example of the Soviet science town, a new social formation characteristic of the modern USSR. Among Soviet towns of this kind, Novosibirsk Akademgorodok, a specially planned complex of diverse institutes, is one of the most famous. Fast growth to the necessary "critical mass," and living standards that in the beginning significantly exceeded the national average, helped Novosibirsk Akademgorodok become a highly efficient "factory" of new knowledge in natural science.

Since World War II, several dozen science towns have been built, mostly of the same scale as Troitsk. Some were built under the aegis of the USSR Academy of Sciences, others by powerful military-industrial corporations of nuclear and aerospace profiles. The impressive scientific and technical potential of centers of this kind can noticeably change the routine technological landscape of the former Soviet Union, due to large-scale conversion of defense industry taking place these days.

As an example, we should consider the Moscow region, a zone of about 60 miles in radius, surrounding Moscow city. This area, where about 20,000,000 people live, has the highest population density in the country, about as many as in California. Here are about a dozen science towns, each of which specializes in its own field. They include

- Dubna International Nuclear Research Center
- Chernogolovka, a complex of academic institutes in solid state physics, chemical physics, and theoretical physics, including the famous Landau Institute
- Pushino, an institute of biophysics, biochemistry, and biotechnology
- Lytkarino, an institute of aviation engineering, development of technology and production of optically active materials for laser industry, and fine precision and unique optical manufacturing
- Zelenograd, the largest Soviet center for microelectronics design and production
- Protvino, the largest Soviet center for high-energy nuclear research
- Zhukovsky, a complex of institutes of the aviation profile, including the Central Aerohydrodynamics Institute
- Kaliningrad, aerospace center for the Soviet "shuttle" and control station
- Dolgoprudny, the largest Soviet educational center in physics and technology, primarily for the defense industry.

This list could easily be continued, but let us return to Troitsk, which will help us consider the advantages and disadvantages of concentrating research potentials at one site.

Building their institutes in Troitsk, the Academy of Sciences and Ministry of Atomic Energy and Industry cared not only about having large research complexes, such as Tokamak, the largest in the former USSR, but significant efforts were also made to prepare highly educated employees for these institutes. The main role here is played by the Moscow State University, the Physics Engineering Institute, and the Institute of Physics and Technology. The graduate and undergraduate students of these institutes study not only in auditoriums, which is usual for other Soviet universities, but they also study directly in Troitsk. In this way scientists-to-be can feel the atmosphere of intensive scientific research in real laboratories.

The children in Troitsk are eligible to attend free preschools and kindergartens in the neighborhood. These schools are well equipped with everything needed for comprehensive education such as music, physical education, computers, and foreign language materials. Full secondary education is also totally free and mandatory. The children's computer and informatics club Bytic with its more than 250 state-of-the-art computers is a place of great popularity in Troitsk. Bytic is not only an educational facility, but also the center of international relations. For three years, Troitsk has participated in active student–teacher exchange programs with different countries, particularly the United States. In 1989, more than 220 students and their teachers from the United States and West Germany spent three to four weeks with Soviet families in Troitsk. The same number of Soviet children and adults traveled abroad, more than half of them to the San Francisco Bay area.

These programs, which have grown into long-term teacher and professional exchanges, have had a great impact on changing human psychology, which in both countries has for years been formed under fear of the future. Our children provide examples for us of how easy and natural our communication can and should be, especially when facilitated with modern telecommunications. Using electronic mail and video telephones, we can daily communicate with our friends half the world away.

All of this allows us to hope that the professional level of the new generations of Troitsk citizens will correspond to the needs of the future. On the other hand, this means that much of today's Troitsk infrastructure will not satisfy the demands of the emerging city. Even today we see limited jobs for our youth who are well educated in the fields of computer design and software development. This necessitates appropriate expansion of the manufacturing facilities and establishment of cooperation in international production and trade.

We have already made initial steps in this direction. Several of our hardware and software engineers work on contracts for U.S. companies. Recently we have started a corporation in the United States, Trinity Kurchatov Science and Technology, Inc. Its main purpose is to commercialize our advanced technology products in the American market. Bechtel Corporation is well known in the former USSR, and we are proud to be among their first Soviet partners. The goal is to create the first Soviet technopolis at Troitsk. The project is viewed as a prototype for future technopoles in the former USSR. Our common global vision of the evolutionary trends in technology and relevant social and industrial structures makes our joint work not only fruitful, but also pleasant.

What is still more important is our common understanding of the necessity to radically and urgently modernize the Troitsk infrastructure to realize the creative potentials of individual scientists, designers, or small R&D and production companies. This is a difficult challenge within the established framework of large institutes, which are best suited to extra-large projects.

The necessary changes in Soviet laws facilitating "small business" operation have already been passed. These immediately released the potential of structures that had been hidden before. In 1989, small business in Troitsk increased its activity by the factor of 20 and had more than 10 percent of the city population involved in its projects, resulting in a near 20 percent share in the total Troitsk production volume. Therefore, task one for Troitsk is building additional infrastructure similar to the American business/research park, which would encourage the operation of small enterprises.

Another important task is liquidation of disproportions between the powerful and expensive research base and the insufficient social infrastructure of the town. With this aim in view, our project includes building a modern village of one-family homes with the necessary social facilities, hotel, shopping center, satellite telecommunications center, and hospital equipped with the most modern diagnostic and treatment means including nuclear magnetic tomographs and lasers, as well as a sports complex.

We believe that an important feature of the project is its openness to foreign partners, both at the development stage and in the future. Today, Soviet laws allow foreign parties to be co-owners or customers of the facilities to be built. We're sure that the most sagacious will take advantage of these new opportunities. In our opinion, the Troitsk technopolis will definitely contribute to natural integration of the former USSR into the world community.

Part Three

Fast Systems: Technology Breakthroughs and Human Resources to Accelerate High-Technology Development

9

The Information Infrastructure in Technopolis: The Intelligent Network

Frederick Williams

Information technologies, like other infrastructure components, are advancing the design of cities of the future. Probably the most traditional information technology component of urban infrastructure is the telephone network, which is rapidly expanding in capacity and uses. We are seeing the emergence of not only a high-capacity voice, data, and image telecommunications network, but also a coalescence of computing and telecommunications—the "intelligent network."

Networks are a mix of transmission and switching technologies. Switches in the intelligent network are sophisticated computers that take on additional chores of network management, including most efficient message routing, accounting, and trouble shooting. In turn, these computers can link with computer-based services for database access, computation, simulation, text messaging, and information services.

Transmission in the intelligent network is a digital rather than analog form, thus allowing mixes of voice, data, and image on the same channel. The transmission "backbone" will likely be broadband fiber-optics, and sometime later "photonic" (light-based) switches will alleviate the costly necessity to interface optical transmission with electronics for switching. Uses of the intelligent network will be limited more by our lack of imaginative application rather than by transmission or switching capacities.

Whereas we often thought of the traditional telephone network as "keeping up" with urban development, the intelligent network is creating new options for the development and design process itself. For example, the network allows industries to decentralize yet stay closely managed. Manufacturing and warehousing operations may be moved to less expensive land and labor forces, design to centers of creativity, final manufacturing closer to markets, and headquarters adjacent to financial districts. This decentralization would not be possible without the advanced telecommunications links that allow management coordination of company operations. Employees may now work in decentralized offices nearer to their homes or in an office in the home, both linked to central headquarters over an intelligent network.

So, too, does the intelligent network bring new options for public services and communications in the home, including applications for education; medical emergencies; security; telemetering of utilities; entertainment; and a variety of voice, data, and publication (facsimile) communications services.

The intelligent network will be the central nervous system of the coming technopolis.

CURRENT NETWORK PROVIDERS

The United States, as are most industrialized countries, is already served by large and complex telecommunications networks. Usually this refers to both the "public switched network" and the private networks. The public network includes local-exchange and long-distance service providers, the former still regulated as a monopoly (the divested Bell operation companies, large independents, and many small rural exchanges), and the latter open for competition, except for the ongoing process of deregulating AT&T so as not to stifle the growth of competition offered by visible contenders such as MCI and U.S. Sprint, plus many small "interexchange" service providers. We use public networks every day to speak on the telephone or to send a facsimile message, a TWX, a Telex, a video image or a computer signal. These are called "common carriers" because they are a network presumably available to all.

"Private networks" may range from local-area networking (LANs) connecting voice and data points within an organization to exclusive longer-distance point-to-point services that link decentralized company components, suppliers, or other associates. Private networks vary between being based on the lease of private lines from public companies or where the network is built and owned by the user. When private networks substitute for use of public ones, this takes revenues off of the latter network, thus possibly raising the "base" cost for public users, a practice called "bypass" and controversial in current U.S. regulatory debates.

A wide variety of specialized, virtually private, "scientific" networks can be accessed by universities, industrial research facilities, and government laboratories or offices. There is an informal hierarchy of these networks, descending in size from the overarching common-carrier networks that carry voice and data around the globe to the specialized international data networks to the regional- or wide-area networks (WANs) and to LANs. In the latter part of this chapter, I describe current trends in the development of scientific networks, for they represent trends in intelligent network development.

TELECOMMUNICATIONS AS A STRATEGIC INVESTMENT

For years, telecommunications—usually thought of as basic telephone service—received little attention beyond its identification as a utility like water, power, or the public roadways. Costs of telecommunications were treated as overhead by most organizations. Given adequate services, most organizations limited their concern with telecommunications to keeping the costs down. Public investments in telecommunications systems took on the nature of a public utility operated either by the government, as in most countries, or by a regulated public corporation in the United States. But today we are witnessing a revolutionary change in the importance of telecommunications. This is not only in the rapid growth of the technology (digitalization, convergence of voice, data and image transmission, inclusion of computing services), but also in the many applications of telecommunications for growth and development, including recognition as a critical infrastructure component for information-age cities or technopolies.

As a consequence of the rapid advancements made in telecommunications and computing technologies and with their integration into modern businesses and service organizations, we are encouraged to regard telecommunications more as a strategic investment. We are challenged to make investments in telecommunications for specific purposes, ranging from the creation of new businesses or the revitalization of traditional ones to the undertaking of urban or national development. Such a challenge reflects the transformation of telecommunications from a taken-for-granted utility like water or power, where the main concerns are low cost and availability, to telecommunications as an investment in competitiveness, productivity, or economic development. It is an attitude whereby we expect a return on an investment. Our success in this investment will be gauged not only in traditional terms of productivity, but also in competitiveness—in the ability of technopolies to compete for economic development in the growing information age economy (Schmandt, Williams, Wilson, & Strover, 1990).

GROWTH IN APPLICATIONS

If we expect organizations to invest in telecommunications with particular purposes in mind, it is necessary to determine how those purposes may be achieved. How does telecommunications add value? The answer is complex, not because the processes are complex but because the effects of telecommunications investment must be seen in concert with other factors. Modern telecommunications planners often say that rather than directly contributing value, telecommunications "facilitates" the development, manufacture, or sales of products, as well as the delivery of services (Dordick & Williams, 1986).

Figure 9.1 illustrates the telecommunications-intensive environment of many of today's large businesses. Information technologies that became linked within the organization in the 1960s and 1970s (e.g., accounting, transactions processing,

Figure 9.1. Expansion of organizational networks.

manufacturing control, record keeping, and word processing) have now been extended through the external telecommunications network to links with suppliers, subcontractors, financial services, and customers. The business literature now abounds with examples of companies that achieved new, competitive positions by innovative use of telecommunications networks.

We can also gain an understanding of the uses of current and advanced networks by examining some of their most popular and anticipated uses, as summarized in Figure 9.2.

RETURNS ON INVESTMENT

Infrastructure Development

On a general level, we can ask how an improved telecommunications infrastructure enhances economic development. Telecommunications researcher Hudson (1984) made the valuable point that many benefits of telecommunications go beyond individual users or organizations to contribute to society and the general economy. Most available studies in this area reflect developing countries and rural economies rather than advanced industrial societies. For example, telecommunications

- Improve overall effectiveness of the management of businesses
- Improve governmental administration and service delivery
- Decentralize business and industry
- Benefit the consumer population with more information and services
- Expand travel and tourism through reservation services

Typical Basic Services
- Electronic mail (messages from one person to another)
- Bulletins (messages from one person to many)
- News (messages from many to many)
- Conferences (conversations between a few or many)
- File transfer (movement of computer files from a source)
- Computation
- Database access and search function
- Encryption (encoding) and security protection (passwords)
- Directory service (similar to a white-page telephone book)
- Gateways or interconnections to other networks or databases.

Advanced Services
- Video conferencing (compressed video or full-scan video, one-way, two-way, multiways with video picture or audio-only response)
- Computer graphics (computer-aided design, modeling, and other advanced graphics in color)
- Parallel computation requiring parallel computers
- High-level computation requiring supercomputers
- Simulation (e.g., weather, astronomy) requiring supercomputers.

Source: Williams, F. *The New Telecommunications: Infrastructure for the Information Age*. New York: The Free Press, 1991.

Figure 9.2. Examples of network services.

- Enhance production by improved ordering and the availability of marketing information.

For infrastructure in general we can envisage both business and human services applications of telecommunications. The quality of life in a technopolis may be as important in the long run as its economic viability.

Attraction or Retention of Businesses

One practical way to look at telecommunications investments is from the perspective of urban economic development programs (Schmandt, Williams, Wilson, & Strover, 1990). Industrial recruitment is central to traditional city economic development programs, although cities have developed a variety of new initiatives. Given that much of the new city economic development activity was stimulated by the closing of manufacturing plants, successful industrial recruitment generates much good will for policymakers. Beyond good politics, however, city concern with manufacturing is sound economics. Even though the service sector in the United States accounted for 95 percent of new jobs from 1970 through 1984, service jobs exist, to a large extent, as a consequence of manufacturing jobs (Noyelle, 1987).

In many cases, the service branch of a firm, like its manufacturing facilities, need not be located near corporate headquarters. This is now made possible in part by advances in telecommunications systems. Cities that are aware of a company's decision to expand its service branch can attempt to keep the service branch nearby. Alternatively, cities can try to lure service branches away from the corporate headquarters. One of the many strategies cities can use to attract such firms is an advanced telecommunications network (Sherry, 1987).

Telecommunications as a Factor of Production

On a more conceptual level, we can consider telecommunications as a "factor of production." The historical analogy of the railroads and their impact on economic growth helps illuminate the role telecommunications may play. The railroads were vital to American economic growth in the late nineteenth and early twentieth centuries. The production processes of that era required the development of a transportation infrastructure like that of the railroads. Economic growth at the time depended on growing markets and mass production techniques. To take advantage of economies of scale, corporations needed a way to link geographically dispersed demand (Piore & Sabel, 1984). The railroads provided that link. Railroads did not create demand but merely enabled innovations to become economically viable by linking markets and thus permitting firms to realize economies of scale (Fogel, 1964).

Telecommunications serves a similar function in today's economy. The importance of telecommunications, as with railroads, is linked to the nature of production processes. American manufacturing today relies much less on mass production that it once did.

The innovations that telecommunications can support are numerous: computer-aided design and manufacturing (CAD/CAM), education, working at home, and more. Telecommunications will be a crucial part of the infrastructure that will facilitate this revolution. These innovations will enable the United States to develop flexible production processes, seen by many as the key to American economic revival (Piore & Sabel, 1984). Because the United States can no longer compete in mass-produced goods, it must compete in technologically evolving markets in which quality, rather than price, is most important. Producers must be able to respond quickly to changing markets; the time between design, production, and sale must be substantially reduced. Engineers and sales people must interact constantly to ensure responsibleness to the market. Quick and efficient communication is the key to making such a process function well. The changing economy is leading the demand for new telecommunications services. How and when these services will be available is directly influenced by the public policies that affect telecommunications.

Applications for Research and Technology Transfer

Telecommunications networks can greatly benefit the research process, as well as bring technology from the laboratory to the marketplace ("technology transfer"). For example, networks can

- Link scientists on "collaborative" research networks
- Link scientists with university, business, and government organizations
- Attract R&D or high-tech industries to a city
- Hasten the technology transfer process by linking laboratories, venture capital interests, and businesses
- Support the delivery of continuing education in engineering and the sciences
- Improve library services
- Enhance educational programs in universities and secondary schools and eventually primary schools. (Williams, 1991)

Telecommunications networks enable geographically dispersed researchers to consult and confer in "real time" with colleagues around the world (Williams & Brackenridge, 1990). These networks provide the link to vast libraries of data and to powerful computation capabilities of supercomputers. Researchers are able to leverage their resources by sharing expensive equipment, such as radio telescopes, with an entire "invisible college." Obscure information once stored within the confines of a single isolated library is now available on-line, worldwide to all who are connected to the network. Simulations and calculations of inaccessible phenomena such as the process of superconductivity or the collisions of neutron stars, requiring the fastest supercomputers, are now available to academic, industrial, and governmental scientists.

We are also seeing the linkage of university, government, or commercial offices concerned with technology transfer as a function into the network. This may be a newly organized university office charged with promoting commercialization of campus laboratory inventions where the network provides mail services to faculty scientists, assists in creating proposals, or offers a database that tracks university research activities. A city government office may use the same linkages to promote its operation, while also using the network to stay in touch with federal laboratories or the agencies publishing requests for proposals.

A research consortium can link itself to all participating groups, scientists, government offices, and its own sponsoring organizations or "shareholders." A shareholder company may see a market opening that could be communicated on the network to a consortium whose staff many in turn use the network to scan university laboratories for relevant research activities.

GROWTH OF HIGH-PERFORMANCE SCIENTIFIC NETWORKS

Computer-Based Networks

Perhaps most relevant to the development of the technology-based economic activity of the coming technopolies are today's high-performance computer-based networks used mainly for linking research institutions. Many of these began life or currently continue as "computer" networks that are telecommunications systems (transmission facilities, switches) dedicated to linking users to computers and computers to one another. The most frequent and well-known application is for user "logon" from terminals, workstations (or personal computers equipped for "terminal emulation") to computers that provide computation, database, or communications services. It is increasingly common for such services to involve logging into a network of computers through a "switch," then connecting users to the computer selected for the particular application. It is this network switching or gateway function that is particularly important because it supports such applications as electronic mail and messaging, file transfer, and access to databases ranging from specialized bibliographic services to electronic journals.

The above services are often divided into two broad categories: computer-mediated communication and resource-sharing services. Either of these may be delayed (batch) or immediate (interactive). Batch computer communication services generally include one-to-one (mail), one-to-many (bulletin boards), and many-to-many (news) services. Interactive computer communication services are instantaneous and immediate with no delay between messages. By contrast, resource-sharing services are based on remote connection (remote logon or the ability to access another computer as if logged onto it locally) and file transfer. Other services include interconnections (gateways) to commercial or international networks, videotext (an interactive system for accessing a wide variety of databases), and user support. Resource sharing will eventually involve group word processing, editing, and publication services, with participation by various users of the network regardless of their geographic location.

Today the primary challenge of large computer networks is to combat problems with incompatibility in order to create connectivity among diverse smaller networks. A multitude of protocols (for example, using IBM, DEC, or others), machine architectures, operating speeds, and capabilities create a nightmare of incompatibilities that isolate groups of users from each another. Major research networks can be likened to a geodesic dome that permits interconnection between these groups of users running on different standards.

Also to be anticipated as networks become more intelligent are new kinds of software for analysis such as an expert system that uses facts and rules of judgment, expert decision making, and logic to find lines of reasoning leading to answers or solutions. New goals for networking include

- Increase research productivity by improving access to information, supercomputers, and other specialized sources

- Advance the quality of academic research and instruction by expanding opportunities for collaboration and cooperation
- Shorten the time required to transmit basic research results from campuses to the private sector and thus enhance national research and product-development capability
- Broaden the distribution of scholarly opportunity and creativity by connecting faculty, students, and staff from diverse geographies. (Williams, 1991)

In all, the scientific networks provide an ongoing example of the sophisticated application of telecommunications for strategic ends. Several such networks are described next.

Internet

Internet, a worldwide internetwork of some 700 local, regional, national, and international networks, links 500,000 users at university, industry, and government research sites. The network acts both as a facility to share resources between organizations and as a test bed for new innovations in networking. There are two Internet network groups based on two protocols: Internet, which uses the TCP/IP protocol, and DECnet Internet, which uses Digital Equipment Corporation protocols. Many institutions belong to both.

The oldest network in Internet is ARPANET, the U.S. Department of Defense Advance Research Project Agency's experimental packet-switched network introduced in 1969. ARPANET is phasing out in 1990. Its traffic will be carried by NSFNET (National Science Foundation Network). NSFNET, one of Internet's major constituents, swill become even more important to advanced research activities.

NSFNET

Figure 9.3 shows a map of the main trunks of NSFNET, a national network created to improve communications, collaboration, and resource-sharing in the science and research community. NSFNET interconnects major regional networks at 250 universities and research sites (Wulf, 1989) and provides any recipient of an NSF grant with access to a supercomputer. The network has three levels:

1. Backbone supercomputer sites consisting of six NSF-sponsored supercomputer centers interconnected on long-haul, high-capacity trunk lines
2. Mid-level networks connected to the backbone and to other mid-level networks and international networks
3. Campus networks

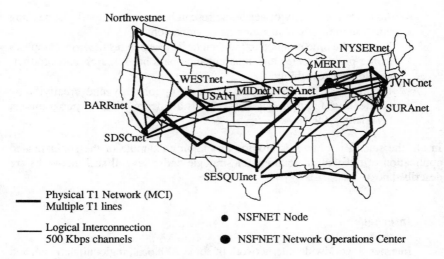

Figure 9.3. Map of NSFNET's major nodes.

The NSFNET backbone uses MCI's fiber-optic circuit and digital microwave radio network to carry data. The management and operation of NSFNET's backbone is supervised by MERIT Inc., a nonprofit consortium of eight Michigan universities (LaQuey, 1989).

Eight mid-level networks are independent entities in a federation linked to the NSFNET backbone. An additional eight networks complete the mid-level group. Among the NSFNET international networks connected through mid-level members are EASINET (European Academic Supercomputer Initiative), JANET (Joint Academic Network) in the United Kingdom, and JUNET in Japan.

BARRNET operates on the second level of the NSFNET and connects universities and research organizations in northern California. Universities (such as Stanford and four University of California northern campuses) and industrial research members (such as SRI International, Hewlett-Packard, Xerox PARC, and Apple Computer) share the network with several government and private research laboratories (such as Lawrence Livermore National Laboratory, NASA Ames, and Monterey Bay Aquarium Research Institute).

THENET (Texas Higher Education Network) provides statewide service to Mexico and to fifty members including universities (such as the seventeen campuses of the University of Texas System, Texas A&M, and Rice University), industrial research members (such as Lockheed, Schlumberger, and Texas Instruments), and other organizations (such as SEMATECH, Microelectronics and Computer Technology Corporation, and Superconducting Super Collider Laboratory). THENET functions in a joint cooperative effort with SESQUINET, a mid-level network connected to the NSFNET backbone. The Texas networks combined form one of the largest of the regional networks and include 2,000 nodes.

These and other networks will play increasingly important roles in fostering interinstitutional exchange within and among cities and eventually technopolies.

NYSERNET

NYSERNET (New York State Education and Research Network), a direct example of network investment for economic development, is one of the six major centers forming the backbone of NSFNET. It is a high-speed data communications network linking universities, industrial research laboratories, and government facilities in New York State. The goal is to give greater access to computing and information resources that will aid in improving economic competitiveness (*NYSERNET News*, 1987). NYSERNET is a nonprofit company formed in 1985 by a group of New York educators, researchers, industrialists, and NSF. Among the forty-seven users of NYSERNET are Columbia University, New York University, Polytechnic University and Cornell University, IBM, Kodak, and Brookhaven National Laboratory. The Cornell National Supercomputer Center and the NorthEast Parallel Architecture Center supply electronic library access and additional network services to NYSERNET (Quarterman, 1990).

Projects promoting technology transfer are daily occurrences at NYSERNET. Four examples of technology transfer are the Apple Computer-University of Rochester connection; the Hartford Graduate Center-NorthEast Parallel Architecture Center connection; the Alfred University-Cornell supercomputer connection; and the State University of New York at Buffalo-Ames Research Center connection.

DEVELOPMENTAL TRENDS

Expansion Orientation

Advanced networks are increasingly far reaching in design so as to encourage use of telecommunications for sharing information, education, experimentation, and most of all, collaboration on new ideas and new products. The days of the solitary inventor or isolated laboratory are almost gone. Groups such as Starlink, the British astronomy network, and OCEANIC, the ocean research group's database, have united researchers with common interests. Consider the Swedish participation on NORDUNET. In two years the Swedish infrastructure grew dramatically to include virtually all higher education institutions and many corporations and government entities, spearheaded by an aggressive national policy.

The promise of advanced telecommunications is new as are the methods of collaboration with electronic tools that can span geographic, cultural, and technical distances. These tools hold the potential to accelerate technology transfer and to enhance its efficacy; we have only to look for ways to improve cooperation—to work together to make optimum use of these networks.

Toward a U.S. High-Performance Network

In the fall of 1989 a plan for a federal high-performance computing (HPC) program was transmitted to Congress by President Bush's Office of Science and Technology Policy. Earlier in 1990, Senator Albert Gore, Jr., introduced legislation proposing the project. Included in this plan is a proposal for the National Research and Education Network (NREN), a federally coordinated government, industry, and university collaboration "to accelerate the development of high-speed computer networks and to accelerate the rate at which high-performance computing technologies, both hardware and software, can be developed, commercialized and applied to leading-edge problems of national significance. . . ." (D. Allen Bromley in the transmittal letter of the Federal High-Performance Computing Program). The goals of the program are to

- Maintain and extend U.S. leadership in high-performance computing, and encourage U.S. sources of production
- Encourage innovation in high-performance computing technologies by increasing their diffusion and assimilation into the U.S. science and engineering communities
- Support U.S. economic competitiveness and productivity through greater use of networked high-performance computing in analysis, design, and manufacturing. (Executive Office of the President, Office of Science and Technology Policy, 1989)

The HPC program stresses increased cooperation among business, academics, and government in building a network that will serve as a prototype for future commercial networks. In proposing NREN, government sources found that the current national network technology does not adequately support wide-based scientific collaboration or access to unique sources, and often the national networks in the United States stand as barriers to effective high-speed communication. Furthermore, Europe and Japan are moving ahead aggressively in a variety of networking areas, surpassing the current state-of-the-art technology in place in North America.

NREN would be built on the existing infrastructure of long-distance lines and fiber-optic cables and would use new transmission technologies to increase its speed and interconnective ability. NREN's structure, based on the existing informal tier system, would be composed of a federally sponsored "super highway" providing support for large users and access for every state; a middle tier of regional and state networks with a broadband capability; and a lower level of smaller networks such as LANs at universities (Gore, 1989).

This supercomputer highway would connect government, academia, and industry with a network ultimately capable of transmitting 1,000 times more data per second than current networks. Three stages are proposed. In the first stage, the existing Internet (T1) trunk lines will be upgraded to 1.5 megabits per second, a project already under way. As a complement to this, DARPA is undertaking a project called Research Internet Gateway to develop policy-based routing mechanisms that will allow the interconnection of these trunks. Additionally, directory services and security mechanisms are being added.

In the second stage, upgraded service will be delivered to 200 to 300 research facilities with a shared backbone network operating at 45 megabits per second. The ability to share this backbone network will reduce costs and improve service. Once the new research backbone is interconnected with the existing NSFNET backbone to and from NREN, it is anticipated that every university and major laboratory will be interconnected.

Third-stage plans are still being developed, but extremely high-speed 1-3 gigabit networks supported by fiber-optic trunks will be important. Also targeted are advanced capabilities such as remote interactive graphics, nationwide data files, and high-definition television (HDTV).

Comparing the network to the interstate highway system built in the 1950s, the initiative could eventually lead to a "wired nation" where small businesses and homes would share in the capability of HDTV, vast electronic data banks, and other applications.

CHALLENGES IN DEVELOPMENT AND DIFFUSION OF THE INTELLIGENT NETWORK

A widely available public intelligent network will take far more effort than the scientific networks just discussed. In many countries of the world, the network will be built by PTTs (post, telephone, and telegraph branch of government), PTTs in alliance with private enterprise; or in countries where telecommunications are largely commercial enterprises, by telecommunications companies. In many of the former cases, the network will be developed when governments put that priority in place.

With one important exception, in the latter cases, building the network will evolve as it becomes a promising business proposition. That exception, and an American example, is that regulatory restrictions hamper the development of new networks. For example, the seven divested Bell holding companies, each of which operates local-exchange companies in designated areas, are barred from originating network information services, with a few exceptions are not allowed in the cable-television business, and cannot connect customers across operating area boundaries. This hinders seven U.S. telecommunications companies, each in the $10-$15 billion range, from aggressively developing the intelligent network, and for many in markets that would promise a decent return on investment. The nation's largest long-distance provider, AT&T, has been barred from information services for the seven years since divestiture and now plans to enter the market aggressively, although they will have to share some proceeds with the local-exchange companies to connect with local customers.

The regulatory environment in the United States in not currently encouraging development of the intelligent network.

User Interface

The exchange of commands and information between the user and the network is probably the weakest link in the intelligent network as it is now being developed. This refers to screen displays, menus, keyboards, the mouse, and lack of natural interfaces that could "see," "hear," and "interpret." One still has to type to convey linguistic information to the computer-based operations of the network; voice input exists in some forms, but the time when the network will detect the critical linguistic features from an awesome variety of acoustic variables and individual differences is still in the future. The Macintosh screen and more recently "Windows" for IBM standards-based personal computers is much improved over old-fashioned, complex, alphanumeric commands, but it is still light-years from being as easy as two people conversing in natural language.

User Implementation

Whereas user skills can compensate somewhat for the interface barrier (i.e., we can learn to type faster or work the mouse), there still is the major problem of using the network in a manner that maximally benefits our personal and professional lives. For example, it is beginning to look as if we are going to make as poor use of computers in the education of our children as we have with television. We have not restructured curricula to capitalize on the power of the computer as a teacher and individualizer of instruction. And at the same time, this lesson—the use of computers for applications—goes undemonstrated for our students.

It is an increasingly accepted generalization that it is the users rather than the designers that "invent" the most effective applications of information technologies. It was clever design engineers who saw and drove the development of CAD uses of computers more so than software writers. Or computer-using editors and writers were the key influence in the increased sophistication of word processing programs. Although much progress has been made, we still travel with many inefficiencies and unrealized opportunities because of the lack of the "final mile" adaptation of our work to the advantages that information technologies can offer, and this transfers as a barrier to full use of the intelligent network.

THE EQUITY CHALLENGE: TOWARD A
NEW DEFINITION OF UNIVERSAL SERVICE

A final point and one that truly should receive more emphasis in the current discussion is the availability of the intelligent network to the full range of citizenry. The telephone business has long been influenced by the concept of "universal service." Although definitions vary, the concept generally means that it is in a national interest to make telephone service widely and inexpensively available. This was AT&T President Theodore Vail's brilliant agreement with the U.S. government when he set a policy of his company bringing the telephone to as many Americans as possible in return for the protection of monopoly status.

Somehow as intelligent networks evolve, we must bring the promise of universal service to all of the citizens of the new technopolies. Otherwise we will be creating infrastructure components that hinder rather than encourage democratic processes. This may be a more important consideration than any of the technical goals in the application of intelligent networks to urban infrastructures.

NOTES

The section on advanced networks in this chapter is taken in part from "Transfer Via Telecommunications: Networking Scientists and Industry" (co-authored with E. Brackenridge). In F. Williams and D.V. Gibson (Eds.) *Technology Transfer: A Communications Perspective.* Sage Publications, Newbury Park, CA: Sage, 1990, p. 172.

REFERENCES

Dordick, H. S. & F. Williams. *Innovative Management Using Telecommunications: A Guide to Opportunities, Strategies, and Applications.* New York: John Wiley & Sons, 1986.

Executive Office of the President, Office of Science and Technology Policy. *The Federal High Performance Computing Program.* Washington DC: U.S. Government Printing Office, 1989.

Fogel, R. W. *Railroads and American Economic Growth.* Baltimore: Johns Hopkins University Press, 1964.

Gore, A. National High-Performance Computer Technology Act of 1989 Newsletter.

Hudson, H. E. *When Telephones Reach the Village.* Norwood, NJ: Ablex, 1984.

LaQuey, T. L. *Users' Directory of Computer Networks Accessible to the Texas Higher Education Network Member Institutions.* Bedford, MA: Digital Press, 1989.

Noyelle, T. *Beyond Industrial Dualism: Market and Job Segmentation in the New Economy*. Boulder, CO: Westview Press, 1987.

NYSERNET News. Troy, NY: NYSERNet, vol. 2, no. 8 (July/August) 1989.

Piore, M. J. & C. F. Sabel. *The Second Industrial Divide*. New York: Basic Books, 1984.

Quarterman, J. S. *The Matrix: Computer Networks and Conferencing Systems Worldwide*. Bedford, MA: Digital Press, 1990.

Schmandt, J., F. Williams, & R. H. Wilson (Eds.). *Telecommunication Policy and Economic Development: The New State Role*. New York: Praeger, 1989.

Schmandt, J., F. Williams, R. H. Wilson, & S. Strover (Eds.). *The New Urban Infrastructure: A Study of Large Telecommunication Users*. New York: Praeger, 1990.

Sherry, M. "Let's Demystify the Service Sector," *Economic Development Review*, vol. 1, no. 4 (Winter), 1987.

Smilor, R. W., G. Kozmetsky, & D. V. Gibson. "Creating the Technopolis," IC^2 Working Paper. Austin, TX: IC^2 Institute, The University of Texas at Austin, 1989.

Williams, F. *The New Telecommunications: Infrastructure for the Information Age*. New York: The Free Press, 1991.

Williams, F. & E. Brackenridge. "[Technology] Transfer Via Telecommunications." In F. Williams & D. V. Gibson (Eds.), *Technology Transfer: A Communications Perspective*. Newbury Park: CA: Sage, 1990.

Wulf, W. A. "Government's Role in the National Network." *Educom Review*, vol. 24, no. 2 (Summer), 1989: 22–26.

10

Managing and Training in the Information-Based Organization

Jerry Richardson

Organizations that will be the most competitive in the 1990s and beyond will be those whose structures, management practices, and training programs add value to the products and services offered their stakeholders.[1] There are three ways of adding value: (1) through the quality of information; (2) through the quality of service; and (3) through the creation of a learning environment. The subject I explore in this chapter is what specific organizational structures and which management practices and styles will most likely be successful in information-based organizations of the future and how the training function can best support those structures and practices.

The organizing principle for organizational effectiveness is simply this: Value added to all stakeholders equals high performance. By "value added" I mean that as a member of an organization the most important thing for a person to keep in mind is, "What ought I to do (now/in this instance) to add value—upward, to my boss; laterally, to my co-workers; downward, to my employees; and outward, to the external world, especially to my customers?"

What is value added? Value added is anything that goes beyond the reasonable expectations of the stakeholder. For example, I am a frequent customer of Nordstrom department stores, a premium retailer of men's and women's clothing, with branches around the United States. One day I was visiting their store in Seattle, where I was scheduled to do a training seminar the next day. A friend and I went to Nordstrom's to pick out a shirt and tie. After being promptly and courteously served, we were talking about the session I was to do the following day while waiting for the shirt and tie to be packaged. The saleswoman overheard our conversation and asked, "Would you like me to have this shirt steamed for you so it will be fresh for your presentation tomorrow?" Impressed, I said, "Yes, of course." "Fine," she replied. "I'll have it taken care of and we'll deliver the shirt to your hotel this afternoon." My friend and I left the store, did some more shopping, went out to dinner, and when we returned to the hotel the shirt, pressed and on a hanger, was neatly hanging in the closet. This is value added. It went well beyond my reasonable expectations and further ensured my loyalty to Nordstrom.

ADDING VALUE THROUGH THE QUALITY OF INFORMATION

Consider how you might add value to the information you provide others within your organization—for example, consider how you provide information to your manager. In my training seminars, I often show participants how to identify the ways in which others process information and make sense of it. You could add value to the information you give your manager by finding out from him or her the following: How, specifically, would he or she like the information packaged? Is your manager the person who likes charts and graphs? If so, then you might put important information in that format. If your manager prefers a narrative written summary of the main points, then your presentation should highlight that. If your manager will be presenting the information to his or her manager, then you might find out how your manager's manager would like the information, so that you can help your manager package the information appropriately. In other words, you add value by helping your manager add value.

In his most recent work, *The New Realities,* Peter Drucker (1989) pointed out that information (rather than mechanization) is now the organizing principle of work. And information technologies are forcing organizations, especially high-technology organizations, to become information based. Information-based organizations will be "composed largely of specialists who direct and discipline their own performance through organized feedback from colleagues and customers" (Drucker, 1989, 207).

One of the most important jobs of these specialists (whom Drucker also refers to as knowledge workers) is to take vast amounts of data and make sense of them. This means converting data into information, both for specialists' own use and for that of upper management, who will use the information to make policy and strategic decisions. (Drucker defines information as "data endowed with relevance and purpose.") Information, then, has value, is something you can do something with, and it adds value to your job.

One of the consequences of this new role of information and knowledge workers is that the bulk of the middle management layer will disappear. Drucker estimates that within twenty years there will be one-third as many middle managers and half as many layers in the organization. The middle levels will disappear because the primary function of middle management has been to transmit information from the top down—primarily in the form of commands and instructions—and to make sure those instructions and commands are carried out in the prescribed manner. All of that changes in the information-based organization, however, because much of the information that upper management will be acting on to make strategic and policy decisions will be coming from the bottom up. And knowledge workers, for their part, resist command and control type structures. To be managed, they need to be led, not by command and control tactics but by practices that add value to their work. Middle managers, unless they can add value either through their leadership or decision-making capabilities, won't be necessary. The middle managers who are kept will be those who have leadership skills and decision-making skills. Managers who neither lead nor make decisions will no longer be needed.

> When an organization focuses its data-processing capability on producing information . . . both the number of management levels and the number of managers can be sharply cut. It turns out that whole layers of management neither make decisions nor lead. Instead, their main, if not their only, function is to serve as "relays"—human boosters for the faint, unfocused signals that pass for communication in the traditional pre-information organization. One of America's largest defense contractors made this discovery when it asked what information its top corporate and operating managers needed to do their jobs. Where did it come from? What form was it in? How did it flow? The search for answers soon revealed that whole layers of management—perhaps as many as six out of a total of fourteen—existed only because these questions had not been asked before. The company had had data galore; but it had always used its copious data for control rather than for information. (Drucker, 1989, 209)

So there is a powerful force at work here to flatten the traditional pyramid-shaped organization: Data is turned into information by cadres of specialists (knowledge workers), who then pass this information directly to top management, often by-passing middle management, who have become redundant. In fat economic times, organizations can afford to carry these people and even to promote them, but in more competitive times when margins are slimmer, organizations need to run leaner and more efficiently.

In high-technology organizations, where global competitive pressures are often felt first, this causes a flattening out of the organization and causes the organization to become lean and mean just to survive. In those environments, if you're not adding value—or aren't perceived to be adding value—you don't last very long.

THE NeXt STEP IN EMPLOYEE INVOLVEMENT

Some firms are taking revolutionary measures to get employees involved in adding value to the quality of the information. At NeXt, Inc., Stephen Jobs is creating what he believes to be a model of the organization of the twenty-first century. Jobs has instituted an "open system" style of management, in which nothing is kept secret from the entire staff, a philosophy of total disclosure.

The pivotal aspect of this process, as one might expect, is the NeXt workstation, which everyone has at his or her desk. These computers are linked to powerful messaging software that Jobs believes will usher in what he calls the age of interpersonal computing. "It flattens out the hierarchy and lets more of the brains in our company participate in decisions," he says. "It absolutely revolutionized our company."

Here's the way NeXt works:

> Notes, decision papers and routine documents are regularly passed around on the network. . . . As a standard feature, the system carries images, as well as voice messages that are retrieved over a high-quality speaker. The interplay, says Jobs, has cut the number of meetings in half while speeding up decision-making. It also makes the chairman more accessible. He receives 350 e-mail messages daily.
>
> But the workstations do more than keep Jobs in touch with his company. They bring the entire staff into the executive suites. For instance, during the first six months of 1989, Jobs was negotiating with Japan's Canon, Inc., maker of NeXt's optical disk drive. At issue was Canon's offer to buy an equity interest in the startup. At most companies, even knowledge of such talks would be confined to a small circle of top executives.
>
> At NeXt, however, Canon's offer, and the controversy it generated, became matters for everyone to debate. In accepting Canon's cash, would NeXt be seen as selling out to the Japanese? For hours each week, the senior staff argued back and forth. After the meetings broke up, executives returned to their groups and recapped the disagreements. The computer network hummed with opinions and counterarguments. And the monthly gathering was all but consumed with ironing out differences and distortions. Finally, last June an accord was struck and Canon purchased 16.7 percent of NeXt for $100 million . . . . (Rothman, 1990; 32)

One of the outcomes that Jobs expects from this open-system management style is to develop managers and leaders more quickly. Everyone participating in the discussion of the highest levels in the organization has the effect of motivating the employees and also serves a training and development function—to model executive decision-making and to expose future managers to the jobs they will be doing someday.

ADDING VALUE THROUGH THE QUALITY OF SERVICE

The rate of change in organizations is rapidly increasing. "Tomorrow" comes faster today than it did yesterday. Organizations that will succeed under these conditions will be those whose structures allow them to respond most flexibly to the changes in the world around them and to the demands of the marketplace in providing the quality products and quality services that customers are increasingly demanding. The most vocal spokesman for this responsiveness under these conditions is Tom Peters.

If the organizing principle for Drucker is information, for Peters it is quality. In his most recent work, *Thriving on Chaos*, Peters (1989) argues that organizations that will thrive will be those that can adjust to and exploit the chaos that is becoming the norm. The most competitive organizations will be those that can most flexibly respond. This will require organizational structures that are flatter and more decentralized.

Peters suggests no more than five layers of management in the largest corporations, preferably with no more than three layers in medium-size companies. He also suggests pruning central staff by getting rid of them or by putting them out in the field in business units. He cites studies that demonstrate that "less is more" when it comes to competitiveness. For example, a 1985 study by the consulting firm A.T. Kearney found that "winning" companies had 3.9 fewer layers of management than "losing" companies (7.2 versus 11.1) and 500 fewer central staff specialists per $1 billion in sales (Peters, 1989).

Like Drucker, Peters (1989) also sees the role of middle and first-line management being forced to change from being command and control cops and disciplinarians to being value-added supporters, facilitators, and advocates for their associates (formerly their subordinates). This will allow the associates to perform most effectively those activities that will provide the highest quality products and services to the customer, who is the most important stakeholder and the one who ultimately determines whether the organization will prosper or fail. The proper function of managers is to solve problems, look for ways to improve working relationships with other departments, and sell their associates' ideas to upper management rather than play politics and other nonproductive corporate games. In other words, their proper function is to add value to their employees by helping them get what they need to do their jobs and not by "supervising" and controlling their work.

By changing the role of supervisors and asking them to look at ways they can add value to the performance of their employees, the number of direct reports can increase significantly. Peters (1989) thinks that it could double the number. Drucker (1989) sees the increase as potentially even greater. In command-style traditional operations, the span of control is about seven, plus or minus two. But in an organization of knowledge workers who depend on feedback from their colleagues and customers (or from the information technology itself), a manager can coordinate the activities of a much larger number of people.

Peters (1989) thinks the self-managing team should become the basic organizational building block. These teams work because the members (ten to thirty per team) get to know each other and each other's jobs and, with proper leadership, can achieve a remarkable degree of cohesion and trust. And this cohesion and trust is the glue that makes the team effective. In fact, Peters believes in this so strongly he asserts that "the power of the team is so great that it is often wise to violate apparent common sense and force a team structure on almost anything" (1989, 302).

DRIVE THE DECISION DOWN TO THE CUSTOMER
CONTACT LEVEL

In 1981, SAS was losing money like other airlines. That year, when Jan Carlzon took over as president, the losses totaled $8 million. Carlzon assessed the situation and realized that his organization was more designed to serve airplanes than to serve customers. It was an organization driven by procedures rather than by service. So he made some drastic changes. Rather than try to be all things to all travelers, as the other airlines were doing, he targeted the business traveler and determined that SAS would focus all its efforts on making sure the business traveler received the best possible service. To make this possible, Carlzon drove the decision-making down to the customer contact level. In effect, he inverted the pyramid. Instead of the employees in the organization supporting their superiors, Carlzon had the revolutionary idea that everyone in the organization should support the people who had direct contact with the customer. This put the customer, in effect, at the top of the pyramid, with top management at the bottom. It was a visible reminder of who is the most important stakeholder in the organization and whose satisfaction ultimately determines the success of the organization, namely, the customer. It worked; in 1983, SAS turned a profit of $71 million while the rest of the industry was continuing to lose money. Adding value through the quality of service, Carlzon proved, is good for business.

ADDING VALUE THROUGH THE CREATION
OF A LEARNING ENVIRONMENT

Among the most detailed and complex studies of the potential of information technologies are those of Shoshana Zuboff, a Harvard social psychologist. Zuboff has coined the term "informated " to describe those organizations that have applied information technology to the process of automation. Zuboff describes this process:

Consider the prototypical example of the industrial robot, which is designed not only to mimic the actions of a human being, but often to resemble the human body as well. In automating a particular part of a production process, that robot also codifies and registers new data about the process. It measures many variables in real time that did not exist before except, perhaps, in the mind of the person who previously did that job. Finally, the robot enables the systematic display and storage of those data in a control room frequently monitored by the very person who had previously worked on the line.
Consider what has happened here: In addition to automating a process, information technology has made that process transparent in a way that it never was before. This is what I call *informating*. (1988)

Zuboff's (1988) main thesis is that information technology offers an unprecedented opportunity to add value to both the processes and outputs of production. At least it offers the potential to add value, if the organization is willing to take advantage of the opportunity. Information technologies, whether they are automating a manufacturing process or a service, create data (potential information) about the dynamics of the process—dynamics that were previously hidden. This data then becomes the source of valuable information which, if people in the organization are trained, allowed, and encouraged to use it, can provide competitive advantages in terms of improving the product, the processes used to manufacture the product, as well as the marketing and distribution of it.

Unlike Drucker and Peters, however, Zuboff (1988) doesn't think that informating will necessarily result in a decline in the population of middle managers, she believes they will still be needed but their function will change. Managers will manage not so much the people as the conditions under which people can learn whatever it is that's necessary to do their jobs. Managers will also "become facilitators of data integration, identifying new interdependences and linkages, developing new ways for the various parts of the organization to generate new synergies" (i.e., new ways to use the information and involve different parts of the organization) (Zuboff, 1988).

But the potential of information technology cannot be realized if top management chooses to use the technology as merely another instrument in the command and control toolbox. If this is the choice, then the potential of the technology can never be realized, because the potential doesn't reside in the technology so much as it does in people's ability to use the technology and the information generated by it. Her advice is to "smarten up the people" rather than to "dumb down the machine." Train people in the "intellective" skills of analytical and procedural reasoning, pattern recognition and problem solving that will empower people to add value to their jobs, their organizations, and their lives. Understanding information becomes a key part of their jobs. Work becomes "in large measure, the creation of meaning, and the methods of work involve the application of intellective skill to data" (Zuboff, 1988; 394).

For Zuboff the organizing principle of work is learning, which is made necessary by the nature of information technology. For you to do your job, you must have the skills to understand information, as well as access to that information. You also must keep up with the continual changes in technology and its uses. Organizational power is contained in the information, and those who are most skillful in learning how to use the information will be empowered.

Properly used, information technology therefore forces new structures and divisions of labor. Instead of hierarchies with rigid lines drawn between the managers and the managed, in the informated organization the leader for today's project might be different tomorrow. The leader of a given project is the one who has the knowledge and skills to coordinate the activities of the other members of the team. These other team members might also be from other disciplines, again depending on the nature of the task to be accomplished. "This does not imply that differentials of knowledge, responsibility, and power no longer exist; rather, they can no longer be assumed. Instead, they shift and flow and develop their character in relation to the situation, the task, and the actors at hand" (Zuboff, 1988; 401–2).

Even if the intention of upper management is to use information technology as a means to maintain control, the nature of technology makes this difficult, if not impossible. As the various processes of an organization become more informated, the resulting database takes on a life of its own. The organization becomes "textualized" and

> the textualization process moves away from a conception of information as something that individuals collect, process and disseminate; instead, it invites us to imagine an organization as a group of people gathered around a central core that is the electronic text. Individuals take up their relationship toward that text according to their responsibilities and their information needs. In such a scenario, work is, in large measure, the creation of meaning, and the methods of work involve the application of intellective skill to data. (Zuboff, 1988; 395)

One implication here is that if you don't like to think, then you're going to have a hard time fitting in to a truly informated organization.

> The informated organization is a learning institution, and one of its principal purposes is the expansion of knowledge—not knowledge for its own sake (as in academic pursuit), but knowledge that comes to reside at the core of what it means to be productive. Learning is no longer a separate activity that occurs either before one enters the workplace or in remote classroom settings. Nor is it an activity preserved for a managerial group. The behaviors that define learning and the behaviors that define being productive are one and the same. Learning is not something that requires time out from being engaged in productive activity; learning is the heart of productive activity. To put it simply, learning is the new form of labor. (Zuboff, 1988; 395)

TRAINING IN THE ORGANIZATION OF THE FUTURE

It is clear that organizational structures and management practices will be changing significantly in the years ahead, driven by a complex combination of internal and external factors. Likewise, training structures and practices must also make the necessary changes. Even though we are moving into waters that to a great extent are uncharted, certain models of excellence do exist to point the way.

The Work in America Institute in Evanston, Illinois has produced an important study of how selected organizations are coping with the introduction of new technology in the workplace. This study included a study of leading-edge training methods practiced by selected American companies. The study produced the following guidelines that other organizations might follow:

- Coordinate training strategy and corporate strategy. Most corporate training is only loosely coordinated with overall strategy (if at all). A senior training person should be involved in formulating corporate strategy. This will help ensure that training is in alignment with overall corporate strategy. Training should also be responsible for communicating corporate strategy to employees and letting them know how the training supports their and the organization's objectives, and by extension, their mutual prosperity.

- Provide continuous learning. What is learned today will have to be modified tomorrow. Management and employees (and their unions) should team up to analyze needs, develop curricula, design training materials, instruct, and evaluate results.
- Train the content experts to deliver training. For example, when line managers are responsible for delivering training, it increases the likelihood that the skills learned will be supported on the job.
- Implement learning by objectives. Get the learners involved in deciding what training they want and need. Also get them involved in the design and delivery of the training. This should include self-paced, learner-controlled instruction and should allow the employee to learn when he or she needs the information or skill, not when it's convenient for the organization to conduct the training. Peer teaching and coaching techniques and strategies should be used, especially with self-managed or semiautonomous teams.
- Establish partnerships with manufacturers (and/or use third-party training organizations). Manufacturers could add value to their products by providing adequate training (at least as an optional add-on). Users could add value by making sure that the employees who must operate the equipment have adequate training in using it.
- Make sure design and delivery of training is cost-effective (and is not done in such a way that makes the most whistles blow and bells ring).
- Link continuous learning and employment security. Retrain rather than rehire (it's more humane and it's usually more cost-effective). (Rosow & Zager, 1988)

MAKE TRAINING SUPPORT THE NEW ROLES AND FUNCTIONS

Self-managing teams need the following skills: leadership, team-building, conflict resolution, communication, problem-solving, time and self management, and cross training to be able to do several different jobs, when necessary.

Managers and supervisors need the following skills: all of the above, plus participative management, group facilitation, decision-making, negotiation and persuasion, and creativity and innovation.

All knowledge workers need intellectual (intellective) skills, which include analytical reasoning, pattern and trend recognition, resourcing, interpreting, problem solving, recognizing trends, procedural reasoning, innovative thinking, learning how to learn, and computer literacy.

Top management needs all of the skills everyone mentioned earlier, plus visioning and strategic planning.

CONCLUSION

We have explored three ways of looking at the future, with a particular focus on how organizations can increase their chances not only to survive but to prevail. For Peter Drucker (1989), information is the organizing principle of work; for Tom Peters (1989), quality is the organizing principle; and for Shoshana Zuboff (1988), it is learning. What they are all pointing to is that our world is changing rapidly, and to survive—indeed to thrive, in that world—we must learn how to create work structures and establish working conditions and relationships that enable us to use our resources in ways that create added value for ourselves, our organizations, our customers and, if we are wise, for our planet. The choices we make today will determine which choices will be available tomorrow.

NOTES

1. I am indebted to my friend Donald Tosti for reminding me of this during a pleasant lunch in San Rafael, California.

REFERENCES

Drucker, P. F. *The New Realities: In Government and Politics/In Economics and Business/In Society and World View.* New York: Harper & Row, 1989.

Peters, T. J. *Thriving on Chaos: Handbook for a Management Revolution.* New York: Knopf, 1989.

Rosow, J. M. & R. Zager. *Training—The Competitive Edge: Introducing New Technology into the Workplace.* San Francisco, CA: Jossey-Bass, 1988.

Rothmann, M. "A Peek Inside the Black Box." In *California Business,* vol. 15, no. 4 (April), 1990.

Zuboff, S. *In the Age of the Smart Machine: The Future of Work and Power.* New York: Basic Books, 1988.

11

Technopolis, Cities, and the Human Dimension: The FAST Program of the Commission of the European Communities

Sten Engelstoft

This chapter has three aims: to describe the general objectives of the FAST (Forecasting and Assessment of Science and Technology) program of the Commission of the European Communities; to answer some basic questions associated with the social and scientific demands related to cities as actors within science and technology; and to elucidate some main research topics and problems associated with science, technology, and cities. The complicated relationship between technological and human factors is stressed.

The objectives of the FAST program of the DG XII (General Directorate of Science, Technology, and Development) within the Commission of the European Communities are to conduct global analyses of the long-term effects of development in science and technology and the interaction of science and technology with the social and economic changes in the European Community as well as worldwide (CEC, 1989). The FAST program focuses on two main tasks:

- To analyze the long-term scientific and technical changes and their implications and consequences for the development of the European communities
- To promote cooperation between research centers in the member countries in forecasting and technology assessment by ad hoc networks.

These two tasks are pursued to achieve the common goal of identifying new priorities for a common research and development policy in the European community. In this respect, particular attention is attributed to the effects of the achievement of the internal market, the improvement of industrial productivity, and the reinforcement of social and economic cohesion of the community. Economic and social cohesion is obviously of great concern within all work carried out in the commission. Major efforts have been made to reduce the differences between regions within the community. Within the FAST program the "Science Technology and Social and Economic Cohesion in the European Community" dossier is of interest. In this dossier it is argued that a community that strengthens its economic and social cohesion is a community promoting cultural, social, and economic interlinkages among the regions and territories that constitute its diversity. In a more cohesive community, the scientific and technological innovation will thus reach a higher level of excellence as it innovates by confronting a diversity of modes (using new technologies and knowledge) in cooperation and exchange (Hingel, 1990). It is worthwhile noticing that the cohesion concept is fundamentally different from the prevailing American "melting pot" philosophy.

The activities of the current FAST program continue the work of previous FAST programs (FAST, 1989) but concentrate on two main themes:

- To study the capacity of European societies to promote the use of science and technology, more in parallel with needs of society[1]
- To study the structural consequences incurred by the globalization of the economy on scientific and technological development in Europe at the level of member states, as well as at the local level of regions and towns.

To achieve the main objective, FAST activities have been broken down in subgroups, one of which is the preparation of the so-called prospective dossiers, (i.e., research documents outlining and ascertaining possible future developments in specific issues).[2] The FAST research actions include

- Forecasting reports (prospective dossiers) on major topics or phenomena of a global character that may extend beyond the strictly European framework
- Applied assessment studies on the implications and consequences of selected scientific and technical developments that present important challenges to society in the future
- Synthesis reports giving a critical analysis of the main forecasting studies published worldwide in specific fields.

In this chapter the main focus will be on one of these prospective dossiers, "The Future of Urban Societies," which has been established to study the prospects of urban societies as individual actors within the promotion and use of policies within science and technology.

URBAN CATCHWORDS

Science-parks and technopolies have become recent catchwords. Urban problems, solutions to these problems, and urban potentials for growth and development are continuously and increasingly attracting the attention of politicians and researchers. For instance, in March 1990, the Danish parliament Folketinget had a one-day debate on the possibilities of strengthening Copenhagen and the Copenhagen region to the possible benefit of the whole nation; and the British House of Commons has recently had a vigorous debate on future investments in traffic solutions in London to improve the functionality of the city.

The growing interest in urban problems can also be detected within the work of various national agencies. Recently, for instance, a new section of urban development has been set up as part of the Dutch TNO Institute (Netherlands Organization of Applied Technology Research) to improve the future possibilities for strategic actions of individual cities.

International organizations also reflect the increasing interest in urban problems. At OECD in Paris, for instance, the "Group of Urban Affairs" has within their new program of urban affairs launched a program on urban impacts of technological and socio-demographic change, a program particularly concerned with possible spatial consequences of new technologies.

Within the Commission of the European Communities the increasing interest in urban problems can be detected by the expanding number of programs dealing with various urban problems. At least four DGs (including the DG XII) are currently involved in major programs concerned with problems relating to urban areas:

- DG V (General Directorate on Employment, Social Affairs and Education) is currently running a program dealing with social urban development, within which economic integration and social insertion of the underprivileged groups of the population are studied.
- DG XI (General Directorate on Environment, Consumer Protection, and Nuclear Safety) is identifying potential policy proposals concerning the physical urban environment, such as air pollution, noise, water quality, and waste disposal.
- DG XVI (Regional Policies) is currently evaluating the importance of cities within the regional development at community level.

This growing interest in urban problems and possibilities raises several important questions, as to what "urban" and "urban problems" mean and how these problems might be solved.

"THE FUTURE OF URBAN SOCIETIES"

The main objectives of "The Future of Urban Societies" have been to design a research program capable of answering questions associated with the social and scientific demands related to cities as actors within science and technology (Drewett, 1990). The study should provide the authorities within the Commission of the European Community with insights into urban change, as well as with a "reading" of the possible evaluation in the functioning of the European urban system and the functioning of the individual cities within this system.

To achieve the above-mentioned goals, FAST is cooperating with a network of researchers on contract and a network of observers. The combined effect of an existing research network—the URBINNO Network (URBan INNOvation research network); a network of independent self-financing observers, the ROME Network (Reseau des Observatoires Metropolitaines en Europe, a European network of metropolitan observers); and a coordinator (the FAST secretariat including the visiting research fellow)—is designed to overcome the traditional gap between researchers and other, politicians, administrators, or planners, (i.e. the "users").

A former mayor of Copenhagen is quoted as saying that either research in urban matters did not tell him anything he did not know or he would not believe it. This is put very bluntly; however, a report from an advisory group on Urban and Regional Planning within the Danish Social Science Research Council (Engelstoft, 1977) concludes that serious problems often arise between researchers and users. From the point of view of the users, it is frequently stated that if results derived from research are to be implemented efficiently, the investigations must be well defined, sometimes even narrow in their scope. Contrary to the users, researchers tend to prefer, or even find it imperative, to design analyses that will ensure valid results of high scientific quality. Furthermore, users tend to prefer normative results that they may reject or act on, whereas many researchers seem to be attracted to establishing and updating databases to improve their knowledge.

The interplay between researchers and users is designed to overcome the above-mentioned problems. The observers have direct access to the research while it is being carried out, and they have a unique opportunity to shape the details of the program. The observers are also able to advise on the desired output, and they will be able to implement new ideas immediately in the individual cities.

SCIENCE, TECHNOLOGY, AND CITIES

The previous FAST programs have identified three priorities for the interplay between science, technology, and society. First, human resources are the core of future growth and innovative capability; second, new dimensions exist in innovation and competition;[3] and third, European science and technology operate within an emerging global economy. Furthermore programs stressed that the innovative capability of Europe is crucial to its future competitiveness and economic integration. It is thus argued that this capability is dependent, all other things being equal, on the degree of anthropocentricity[4] of technological changes, as well as on immaterial investments based on new forms of integration between technologies, skills, and organizational factors. It is recognized that "knowledge" inputs are crucial, particularly as knowledge content in goods and services is increasing. Consequently, there is a growing interest in how and where these knowledge components are produced, distributed, and consumed and whether the milieux necessary to sustain these activities are likely to develop in the future.

Because cities are usually considered to be the principal centers of innovation and diffusion, as well as nuclei of knowledge resources, it is conceivable to regard cities as key actors in science and technology.[5] Not only do the cities produce new science and technology, they also are major consumers. They provide intellectual and physical infrastructure for knowledge (or brain) workers (Gizycky, 1988) and also the cultural and social environment for these workers' personal needs. Thus, the necessary framework for innovations should not be regarded as purely technological; cities are centers of many social, cultural, institutional, and morphological innovations. The latter, however, often interact to add a new quality to the technological change, but they may also constrain it. It is therefore important to understand how the urban milieux can provide for the innovation flux and maintain the quality of the urban living (human) environment. The outcomes will affect not only the competitive position and quality of life of individual cities, but also of European society as a whole.

Within the study of urban-related problems, one has to distinguish between general trends in the development of the urban system (the so-called megatrends or general opportunities) and the individuality of a particular city (the so-called heritage). The general opportunities are constituted of factors related to common tendencies within population dynamics, economic restructuring, and social differentiation, as well as international trends. Heritage is more difficult to define; it is connected to history and tradition—a variety of factors specifically related to a locality.

RESEARCH OBJECTIVES

As a of result of the above-mentioned considerations, the preparation of the research program has become an important part of "The Future of Urban Societies." As the interaction between the researchers and the users has progressed so have the research objectives. In the end, these objectives were found to be contained in two main issues, and these issues correspond to the ideas of opportunities and heritage:

1. Mega trends, transformation, and scenarios
   - European cities in a new historic phase
   - Transformation issues
   - European cities after 1990.
2. Cities as actors in science and technology
   - Innovation and urban milieux
   - Knowledge-based city
   - Knowledge production and consumption
   - Spatial impact of new technology.

Within the framework of "Technopolis, Cities, and the Human Dimension," particular problems related to the individual locality and consequently related to the heritage dimension are of interest. There is a close connection between the heritage concept and the ideas of the FAST cohesion study. The latter stresses the importance of cultural, social and economic diversities among regions and territories as a way to obtain a higher level of excellence within science and technology.

Innovation and the urban milieux imply a thorough study of the innovation concept itself and particularly the linkages between innovation processes and cities and vice versa. The interplay among invention, implementation, and diffusion of innovations is studied in the urban context, and particular attention is given to the links between diffusion and infrastructure (Fox-Prezeworsky, 1989). Examples of innovations (social, cultural, institutional, economic, and technological) are examined. The main focus however, will be on the interplay among innovation, science and technology, and the human dimension. The idea (promoted by Professor Peter Nijkamp of Amsterdam) that the existence of certain critical success factors should be ensured and promoted will be further examined. These success factors could be described as INFOware, ECOware, SOFTware, HARDware, and ORGware. Furthermore, these factors are interlinked to ensure creativity, communication, and competence.

Under the heading of the "knowledge-based city" the idea that certain localities or cities constitute a specific knowledge base (Knight, 1989) or experience, embedded in corporate headquarters, research centers, technical and training centers, universities, commercial firms, as well as the labor force, is developed further. To promote the success of a city this knowledge base should be secured and enlarged, to obtain the institutional and economic base of the firms. The research will develop methods to define and measure the knowledge base of cities. Key actor groups involved in the knowledge production and distribution are to be examined as is the role of cities in developing and accessing knowledge through information service networks using information technology.

Problems related to knowledge production and consumption should be assessed through studies of actual linkages between cities and various actor groups involved in knowledge production (research institutes, universities, and some basic research and development companies) and knowledge use (firms). The latter should be evaluated with regard to of innovations products (material and immaterial) or process (technological, organizational, or managerial).

As mentioned earlier, cities are important consumers of new technologies, and the spatial impact of these should be considered carefully, particularly the technology component of urban services (Illeris, 1989). Local development should be evaluated carefully, as should the consequences for intercity networking through high-speed rail and fiber-optics.

Finally evaluating the possibilities of cities acting individually within science and technology should be attempted. As the effect of the Single European Act[6] and the diminishing importance of the national borders emerge, individual regions and cities will achieve an increasingly important position as decision makers and actors.

This will create new opportunities, but it will also create new problems within cooperation, as well as competition, of the individual cities.

DISCUSSION

Within "The Future of Urban Societies" it is argued that "towns remain major agents of economic, social and cultural change as well as crucial places where major societal problems are expressed . . ." and that in the future, particularly as a result of the Single European Act and the new open markets of 1992, cities will increasingly act individually as decision and policy makers. This acting is expected to happen within all aspects of social, economic, and technological development.

To understand, explain, give policy advice, and act within these new conditions we must know exactly what we are talking of when we mention city-related problems. The city, as we intuitively perceive it, is only a reflection of general societal processes. It is, however, a highly condensed image of these processes (Gullberg, 1981). The city is thus an empirical and not an analytical category; it is an area of immense interest, the perfect example; but there is no such thing as specific urban processes that can add extra individual explanatory power to our understanding of modern society.

It is dangerous to condense several exceptionally complicated relationships into a few (undefined) urban catchwords because this might easily lead to hasty conclusions based on false beliefs in specific metaphysic urban characteristics and problems. Such conclusions might possibly make us overlook complex combinations of several more straightforward explanations.

CONCLUSION

"The Future of Urban Societies" is a research program that attempts to approach urban problems, particularly those concerning cities as actors within science and technology. The importance of the program is in its attempt to disintegrate the problems into individual components, technological as well as human. When this has been done successfully, a complicated process must be entered—comprehending intricate relationships among the components while never forgetting the human component.

If, on the contrary, we subscribe to a process where we search to identify urban processes, the difficulty becomes whether we are not trapped by (understandable) scientific sales-talk that might be comparable to marketing a new detergent: All the news is really in the wrapping, but "it certainly does wash whiter!" Or does it?

NOTES

1. It is important to stress that within the FAST program emphasis is not on development of science and technology as such; the focus is on the interaction between these developments and the interactions with social and economic changes in the community in the light of worldwide developments.

2. Within FAST, the future-oriented research is carried out as prospective research partly by scenario writing: this method (writing scenarios) does not in itself add to our knowledge of the future; however, it does enable us to consider possible alternative futures before choices are made or plans are elaborated (Werf, 1987). Scenario writing is thus in sharp contrast to more traditional mathematical forecasting.

3. By new dimensions of innovations is meant the study of innovations by use and within different modes.

4. An anthropocentric quality of any technology is related to the way it is linked to the human faculties brought into play in the labor process. For a technology to acquire an anthropocentric quality, work must be organized accordingly. A technical system may thus be called anthropocentric if it facilitates human work processes by its very use and in conjunction with the other working conditions. The concept is further developed in a FAST report of "European Competitiveness in the 21st Century" dealing with integration of work, culture, and technology (Cooley, 1989).

5. This somewhat tautological argument seems to constitute one of the key explanations of the recent growing political interest in urban problems. It is founded in the belief in (so far undefined) specific urban processes or characteristics (Andersen & Engelstoft, 1990); this will be dealt with in a later paragraph.

6. The expression "Single European Act" refers to the legislative framework of the Commission of the European Communities that have been designed to ensure the free movement of capital, goods, services, and people within the Community. This is to be achieved by January 1, 1993.

REFERENCES

Andersen, H. T. & S. Engelstoft. "The Material Production and the Urban Concept." In R. Hutchison (Ed.), *Review of Urban Sociology,* vol. 2. Greenwich, CT: JAI-Press, 1990.

CEC. *Information Package MONITOR Programme (1989–1992).* Brussels: Commission of the European Communities, 1989.

Cooley, M. *European Competitiveness in the 21st Century: Integration of Work Culture and Technology.* Brussels: FAST Program, CEC, 1989.

Drewett, R. *The Future of Urban Societies, The Role of Science and Technology, Research Programme.* London: London School of Economics, Department of Geography, 1990.

Engelstoft, S. *Forskning om erhvervslokalisering og regional Udvikling. Arbejdsudvalget vedr. by- & regionforskning (BYREF).* Copenhagen: Statens Samfundsvidenskabelige ForskningsrÜd, 1977.

FAST. *The FAST II Programme (1984–1987), Results and Recommendations; vol.1, A Synthesis Report: Science, Technology and Society; European Priorities.* Brussels: FAST Program, CEC, 1989.

Fox-Przeworski, J. "Concentration of New Information Technologies: Are There Spatial Concerns?" In J. Brotchie, P. Hall & M. Batty (Eds.), *The Spatial Impact of Technological Change.* London: Croom Helm, 1987.

Gizycky, R. von & W. Ulrici. *The Brainworkers.* MÅnchen: R. Oldenburg Verlag, 1988.

Gullberg, A. "Modern Urbanteori. En selektiv presentation." In *HÑften för Kritiska Studier.* Stockholm: Bonniers Publishing, 1981.

Hingel, A. J. *Diversity, Equality and Community Cohesion.* Brussels: Commission of the European Communities, DG XII/H/3, 1990.

Illeris, S. *Services and Regions in Europe.* Avebury, Aldershot: FAST Program, CEC, 1989.

Knight, R. V. "City Development and Urbanization: Building the Knowledge Based City." In: R. V. Knight & G. Gappert (Eds.), *Cities in a Global Society. Urban Affairs Annual Review,* vol. 35. Beverly Hills: Sage Publishing, 1989.

Werf, D. van der. *Work in Europe, Five Possible Scenarios.* Brussels: FAST Program, CEC, 1987.

Part Four

Global Networks and Their Implementation:
Personal, Institutional, and Technological
Networks for Infrastructure Development

12

Personal Networks and Infrastructure Development

Howard E. Aldrich
Mary Ann von Glinow

Today's world is an unsettled place. The four horsemen of the corporate apocalypse—global competition, deregulation, accelerating technological change, and hostile takeovers—are afoot in the land (Kiechel, 1988). But, according to classical economic theory, ambitious business owners thrive on unsettling and turbulent conditions. Their greatest gains are made when discontinuities and gaps appear in society's economic fabric, making traditional modes of doing business or traditional products and services obsolete. Even under normal conditions, hidden opportunities for linking new products or services to untapped markets may be available, if only businesses could obtain information about where they lie.

Business development is a result of, among other things, motivated entrepreneurs and managers with access to resources finding niches in opportunity structures. On the demand side, opportunity structures contain the environmental resources that can be exploited by new businesses as they seek to carve out niches for themselves. On the supply side, motivated entrepreneurs and managers need access to capital and other resources to take advantage of perceived opportunities. In short, business development involves value creation through mobilizing resources in response to opportunities. Central to this formulation is the following proposition: To add value, the people who are involved must create linkages or relationships between key components of the process; in short, they must become involved in social networks.

In this chapter we review some key concepts that help us understand the characteristics of networks and how our access to information is affected by our position in them. We emphasize the difference between direct ties and indirect ties, showing how indirect ties and their strength affect the number of people we can reach in a network (and hence, the value of the network), as well as the diversity in our networks. Networking is heavily influenced by uncertainty, competition, and the social boundaries within which behavior occurs. After discussing how these factors may constrain networking, we examine some strategies for overcoming such barriers. We focus on planning and monitoring network activities and on strategies for increasing network diversity. Our review examines strategies at the individual, organizational, and public policy levels.

WE ARE CLOSER TOGETHER THAN WE REALIZE

How big is the world of business? Consider for a moment how many ties it might take to reach all of the 100 million business managers and owners in the developed world. Some simple mathematics shows that in theory each of us is no more than four steps away from anyone else in the work force. Consider the following example. Think about the number of people on your office Rolodex. Inspection of these sources leads to the reasonable assumption that each of us knows 100 other people, that these 100 people also know 100 people, and so forth. Then, our direct ties include 100 people, and as they each know 100 people, we are two steps away from 100 times 100, or 10,000 people. In three steps, we reach 10,000 times 100, or 1,000,000 people, and in four steps, 1,000,000 times 1000, or 100,000,000 people (Figure 12.1). Obviously, most of us do not perceive that we are so closely linked to the rest of the business community, but the potential is there.

Three constraints limit our ability to extend the reach of our ties: (1) uncertainty—there will be some unknowns between us and a target so that we do not know with whom to start; (2) opportunism and lack of trust on the part of others within our network's reach impose constraints on our willingness to contact others; and (3) social boundaries channel our interactions with others so that we are less likely to meet representatives of some groups—many of the 100 people known to our friends are also known to us, and so our personal networks are somewhat confounded. We address these constraints later.

THE KEY CONCEPTS IN USING NETWORKS

We must distinguish between personal networks and social networks. Personal networks are constructed from the viewpoint of a particular individual, but the social network is much broader; it can include the local community, a region, or an industry. It may even span national boundaries. In examining social networks, we start from a population under study and identify all those connected by a certain relationship. Given a bounded system, we identify all the links between people within the boundaries.

This way of thinking about networks alerts us to the way personal networks either interconnect and overlap or are isolated from one another. People might enjoy extensive connections within a limited region of a total network, but lack the

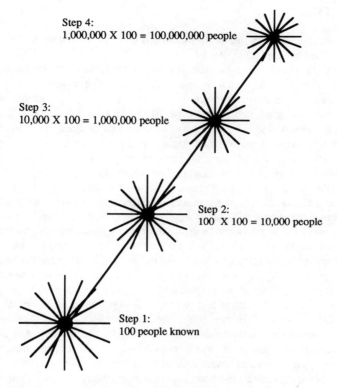

Step 4:
1,000,000 X 100 = 100,000,000 people

Step 3:
10,000 X 100 = 1,000,000 people

Step 2:
100 X 100 = 10,000 people

Step 1:
100 people known

Figure 12.1. Multiplying contacts through networks.

indispensable relationships needed to discover essential information in another region. Information and resources can be thought of as mapping onto networks, and networks can be thought of as the thread or channel along which information and resources flow.[1]

What goes through the ties? Relationships may be treated as containing: (1) communication content, or the passing of information and advice from one person to another; (2) exchange content, or goods and services; and (3) normative content, or the expectations persons have of one another because of some special characteristic or attribute, such as moral support provided by close friends. A personal network, or role set, consists of those people with whom we have direct relationships (or, for some purposes, indirect relationships via direct relationships). For example, for entrepreneurs, we could think of key stakeholders, including partners, suppliers, customers, venture capitalists, bankers, other creditors, distributors, trade associations, and family members.

DIRECT TIES

The simplest personal network includes direct ties linking people with people with whom they have direct contact.

When we use the term *networking* as a verb to describe behavior, we are usually thinking of special relationships within personal networks—a network built on strong ties, relationships entrepreneurs can "count on." By contrast, weak ties are superficial or casual, and people typically have little emotional investment in them (Granovetter, 1973). The strength of ties depends on the level, frequency, and reciprocity of relationships between people, and ties can vary from simple, one-purpose relationships to multiplex, all-purpose relationships. Brief examination of this idea gets at the heart of why networks are important.

Picture behavior at two extremes: first, one-of-a-kind, short-term, nonsustaining transactions between people who never expect to see each other again (e.g., buying a magazine at a corner newsstand in downtown San Francisco), and second, contact between two people who expect to see each other frequently, interact meaningfully, and who are in a relationship for the long term (e.g., taking an R&D consortium manager to lunch to discuss specifications for a new type of equipment you would like the consortia to investigate). The first behavior is a straightforward, pragmatic transaction between people whose personal characteristics are rarely important; in many circumstances, it can be an efficient way of doing business. However, there are three problems associated with these short-term, market-mediated transactions: opportunism, uncertainty, and exit.

First, opportunism is always a possibility. In short-term, nonsustaining relationships, competitive behavior makes perfect sense (Thomas, 1976). Second, this problem is exacerbated under conditions of uncertainty. It may be impossible to predict all the conditions under which a contract must have be carried out or to know precisely all the specifications a piece of equipment will have to meet. Third, when problems crop up, the other party may simply exit (Hirschman, 1972). Whereas you might like to collaborate (Maier, 1973), the other party may simply walk out, leaving you in the lurch.

In contrast, networking refers to the expectation that both parties are investing in a long-term relationship. Consider three benefits that follow from creating a social context in which people expect to deal with each other frequently over an extended period: trust, predictability, and voice.

First, regardless of what popular fiction says about business, trust—assured reliance on the character or truthfulness of someone—is an important component of business dealings. As Thorelli (1986; 47) noted, "networking places a new emphasis on personnel. Power, expertise, perceived trustworthiness, and social bonds are often person-specific rather than firm-specific." Trust is enhanced—purely through self-interest—under conditions when people feel there is a good chance of dealing with each other again. Self-interest is involved because a reputation for reliability and keeping one's word raises the probability that other people will continue to deal with you. As Gee (1981; 15) noted, "the optimal communication mode for successful technology transfer is person-to-person contact."

Second, predictability is increased when long-term relationships are established. Predictability, to some extent, depends on trust. If trust exists in a relationship, then behavior tends to be predictable. The inherent uncertainty in a situation is not reduced. However, based on that trust, what is reduced is the uncertainty about whether the other party will do something to assist you when things do not go according to plan. Uncertainty is also reduced when your network contacts tell you where to go for assistance and provide information or resources you might not otherwise obtain.

Third, people are more likely to use voice rather than exit in response to problems in long-term relations. Voice is making one's complaints known and negotiating over them, rather than sneaking silently away, and is a canon of good problem-solving techniques (Maier, 1973).

Thus, networking with one's direct ties to turn them into strong ties is a way of overcoming the liabilities inherent in purely marketlike transactions with other people. Networking involves expanding one's circle of trust. In network terms, relationships of trust are strong ties, as opposed to casual acquaintances, who are weak ties (Granovetter, 1982).

Indirect Ties

Direct ties, especially strong ones, are significant not only for the people directly linked to you, but also for the indirect access they provide to people beyond your immediate contacts. Including indirect ties takes us closer to the essence of networks, as we begin to see how people can expand their direct connections by the judicious choice of contacts who have access to others. Figure 12.2 shows a business person, labeled A, linked to her direct ties, who in turn are linked to several other people with information or resources of value. In addition to strong direct ties to B, C, and D, shown as solid lines, one of her direct ties is weak, shown as a dotted line to E. Are there only four ties present, or are there really more?

Indirect ties enable entrepreneurs to substantially increase their access to information and resources, multiplying by many times over what is available through their direct ties. We will use Figure 12.2 to illustrate three aspects of entrepreneurs' personal networks: density, reachability, and diversity.

Density. The density of a network refers to the extensiveness of ties between people, and is measured by comparing the total number of ties present to the potential number that would occur if everyone in the network were connected to everyone else. The simplest measure of density considers only the presence or absence of a tie, but more sophisticated measures consider the strength of ties. In

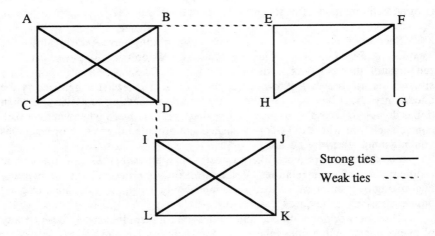

Figure 12.2. Three interconnected personal networks: weak and strong ties.

Figure 12.2, the number of people in entrepreneur *A*'s direct personal network is four, including *A, B, C,* and *D*, and the maximum possible number of ties is given by the formula *(N)*(N-1)/2, or (4)(3)/2 = 6*. (The six ties could be *AB, AC, AD, BC, BD,* and *CD*, if all were active.) As this is also the actual number present—all four persons directly know each other—density is 100 percent. (In the personal network centered on *F*, neither *G* and *H*, nor *E* and *G*, know each other directly, and so density is 4/6 or 67 percent.)

Reachability. Reachability refers to the presence of a path between two people, either directly connecting people known to each other or using direct ties as intermediaries to indirect ties. People can be ranked by the number of intermediaries through which a path travels before one person is indirectly linked to another. Some people are completely isolated from others, as no path links them. For most of us, however, there is a path to many other people, although it may be lengthy. In Figure 12.2, all people have paths between them, with the longest between *G* and *K*—a path of six relationships (*GF, FE, EB, BD, DI,* and *IK*) and five intermediaries.

Short paths are responsible for the often-heard comment "Isn't it a small world?" when two apparent strangers meet and discover they have a mutual friend in common. Think back to the example with which we started the chapter: In theory, we are all no more than four steps away from any other business person in the developed world.

Diversity. Because we are likely to associate with those most like ourself, many of our network members are similar to each other—they have similar personal characteristics and are known to each other as well. The diversity of a network depends on those people different from yourself and is crucial to the scope of opportunities open to you.

You may have a small group of friends you know well, each of whom knows the others well, such as the network centered on person *A* in Figure 12.2. That network is a high-density one. Information known to one person in this group is rapidly diffused to the others, and you learn little from talking to *C* beyond what you already knew from talking to *D*. These people are relatively insulated from the outside, and interaction mostly produces redundant information. Some research on entrepreneurs has found that their strong ties are typically of long duration, extending over ten years or more.

You may also have many casual acquaintances, each of whom also has a circle of close friends, such as person *B's* weak tie to *E* in Figure 12.2. These close friends of your casual acquaintances (*F* and *H*) are unlikely to be known to you, and thus your only possible ties to them are through the casual acquaintance. Thus, if either *F* or *H* has information of value, your only possible access to the information will be through the weak ties.

People with whom we have weak ties, such as casual acquaintances, are less likely to know one another than are people with whom we have strong ties, such as close friends. Therefore, a personal network made up of a person's direct and indirect weak ties will be a low-density network, with many people unknown to each other, whereas a personal network made up of a person's strong ties will be a high-density network, with most people known to each other (Granovetter, 1973). Of course, most personal networks will include a mix of weak and strong ties, and it is the relative balance of weak to strong that is crucial.

Individuals with few weak ties "will be deprived of information from distant parts of the social system and will be confined to the provincial news and views of their close friends" (Granovetter, 1982; 106). Alternatively, having diverse strong ties, such that one's immediate network includes strongly linked people who have ties to different parts of the social system, could provide information channels otherwise unavailable. For example, in Figure 12.2, *D* is strongly tied to *B*, and provides *B* with an indirect channel to *I*, who is in a different network.

Successful networkers are more likely, therefore, to be found in positions connected to diverse information sources. Information about new business locations, potential markets for goods and services, sources of capital or potential investors, and innovations is likely to be spread widely among individuals. Other things being equal, someone with a small set of overlapping ties is at a disadvantage when competing for information with someone with a large set of diverse ties.

SOCIAL SYSTEMS AS NETWORKS

Most concepts necessary to analyze social networks have already been introduced, including density, reachability, and diversity. Three additional concepts are important: centrality, broker roles, and bridges.

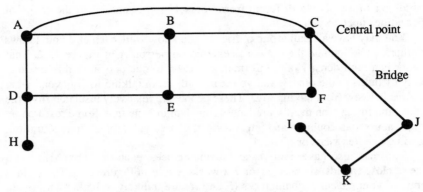

Figure 12.3. Social network: centrality, bridges, and brokers.

Centrality. The centrality of a person in a network is determined by two factors: (1) the total distance from a person to all other people following all paths leading outward from that person and (2) the total number of other people that can be reached. The more people that can be reached and the shorter the aggregate distance to these people, the higher the centrality of a person. Figure 12.3 illustrates a social network, with person *C* in a central role, directly linked to four other people. Person *C* is in the middle of many paths and thus may play several important roles.

People who have extensive ties to different parts of a network can play a key role in infrastructural development. They can serve three important functions: (1) they can serve as communication channels between distant people; (2) they can provide brokerage services linking unconnected parties to each other by transferring resources; and (3) if they are dominant or high-status individuals, they can serve as role models for others or can use their positions to direct the behavior of others. Their central role gives them more power and influence in networks than would otherwise be possible if they had to rely merely on the resources they directly control.

Brokers. Brokers are people who serve as intermediaries. They link people with complementary interests, transfer information or resources, and otherwise facilitate the interests of people not directly connected to each other. For example, venture capitalists are probably as important for their broker role as for the funds they provide to struggling entrepreneurs because they bring together technical experts, management consultants, and financial planners to supplement the entrepreneur's knowledge and experience.

Some social settings facilitate brokerage, and some associations and organizations are themselves brokers in the role they play. Many voluntary associations, trade associations, public agencies, and other organizations increase the probability of people making contact with each other. The complex pattern of social organization in Silicon Valley, California, illustrates the synergistic effects of brokers, central meeting points (bars and restaurants), and family and friendship networks in supporting high start-up rates (Rogers & Larson, 1984).

Bridges. Brokers create bridges. Bridges are links that join two regions of a network that would otherwise have little, if any, contact with each other. For example, in Figure 12.3, there is a bridge between C and *J* that links two otherwise isolated sections of the network. Bridges in social networks play a role analogous to those Kanter (1977) identified in the opportunity structures of organizations; they allow people to leap over otherwise unbridgeable gaps in their development.

Personal networks and social networks are simple but powerful ideas, allowing us to conceptualize the opportunities and constraints facing owners, managers, and policy makers in the pursuit of their goals.

BARRIERS TO INFORMATION FLOW AND TECHNOLOGY TRANSFER THROUGH NETWORKS

We return now to the question implicitly posed by our example of how each of us is potentially only four steps away from 100 million people. What prevents us from easily reaching everyone in the business world? Earlier, we listed three possibilities: uncertainty, competitive behavior, and social boundaries.

Uncertainty and Competition

Uncertainty is a generic problem in economic life, and networking is no exception. The problem is exacerbated when we are dealing with people over whom we have no authority or influence. Transferring information to people whom we do not know on a face-to-face basis—through people as yet unknown to us—is a problem in technology transfer. As Arrow (1962) pointed out, the market for "know-how" is notoriously inefficient, and it is precisely this "know-how" that is critical to successful technology transfers (Von Glinow, Schnepp, & Bhambri, 1991). Under conditions of high uncertainty, people are likely to turn to non-task-related characteristics as a guide to assessing the validity of information (Auster, 1989).

Competition is a problem whenever the other party you are dealing with expects that you are engaged in a one-time transaction, and they will never see you again. It also arises at the start of many transactions that might grow into a long-term relationship and the parties are jockeying for relative advantage. Each national culture has developed ways to deal with the mistrust generated by the possibilities of opportunism. In the United States, businesses rely on lawyers, contracts as thick as phone books, and a high level of secrecy surrounding transactions. In Japan, businesses rely on a series of incremental steps, spending a great deal of time with people from the other side, and the preservation of their business's "face." In

China, the practice of mutual favors, called *guanxi*, is at heart of most business arrangements. "When a contract is negotiated between joint venture partners, it is the *relationship* between the two parties, not the legalities supporting the document, that upholds the contract and prescribes future action" (Von Glinow & Teagarden, 1990; 29).

SOCIAL BOUNDARIES

Social boundaries are perhaps the most pervasive interaction barriers limiting reach and diversity in networks. We refer to the boundaries that groups, organizations, and countries construct around themselves, barriers that thwart interaction with others not within the same boundaries. These barriers include national culture and language, industry differences, organizational commitment and loyalty, and occupational and professional socialization and training.

National culture and language barriers have slowed the impact that modern transportation and telecommunication systems have had on the distances separating people in different regions of the world (Fulk, Rogers, & Von Glinow, 1990; Von Glinow, Schnepp, & Bhambri, 1991). Various institutes and training programs have sprung up to bridge cultural gaps (e.g., between Japanese and American managers), but we suspect that the personal networks of most business people are fairly homogeneous with respect to country of origin.

Within industries, acceptable ways of doing things are taken for granted by most participants. People build their careers within industries and typically develop a high degree of loyalty to them, especially in the West. Within organizations, similar forces lead to high identification and commitment to one's employing organization, especially in Japan. Finally, within many occupations and professions, a common vocabulary and taken-for-granted assumptions, plus long-term career interests, lead to markedly different views of the world.

These factors, among others, create a world fragmented by socially constructed boundaries in which networks build rapidly within boundaries but slowly across them. The boundaries are both the cause and effect of different interests, commitments, vocabularies, world views, and ways of interacting. What are the consequences for networking?

Within social boundaries, a homogeneity of outlook often develops reinforced by strong ties between people that produce a reluctance to risk communicating with outsiders. Or, more often, communicating with outsiders occurs, but misunderstandings arise because people are not aware they have different assumptions, or even world views, and attach different meanings to the same events. Clearly, interaction within boundaries has advantages: Communication is faster and easier within our own circles, and we may find strong emotional and social support for our behavior. However, respecting boundaries too much often leads to missed opportunities and reduced innovativeness.

We must recognize that social boundaries often create tacit or implicit knowledge that we take for granted. People within an industry, organization, or group often know more than they can consciously articulate. As Millett (1990) noted, technologies are not simply hardware and products, and nontechnological knowledge has profound effects on processes such as R&D. This knowledge is embedded in unconscious processes, customs, and traditions. Implicit knowledge is what adds authenticity to local products—whether they are goods, services, or know-how—and makes them hard for outsiders to reproduce. It is also this knowledge that makes networking valuable, to the extent that face-to-face contact reveals the existence of such knowledge to both parties.[2]

For example, when Toyota executives wanted to determine how American consumers actually used their cars, they created research teams to study Americans' life-styles. They "attended a cocktail party in Houston, where they concluded that people preferred a distinctive grille because it made the car more impressive when brought to the door by a valet. They also went to baseball parks, where they measured how close cars were parked to one another, to help decide on sliding doors instead of swing-open doors for mini-vans" (Levin, 1990).

The potential of networking is thus limited by uncertainty, competition, and the presence of many social barriers that constrain information flow. Uncertainty is a generic problem, present to some degree in most social and economic transactions, whereas competition may be partially dealt with by cultural arrangements and negotiations between the people involved (Williamson, 1981). Social boundaries emerge naturally as a product of human interaction and as a deliberate construction by people and groups attempting to limit entry into or exit from some social unit.

HOW CAN THE BARRIERS BE OVERCOME?

What strategic implications follow when considering infrastructure development from a personal network perspective? Can networking be managed? We note that true networking is heavily influenced by chance and the number and level of social boundaries. Public policy makers, owners, and managers can create conditions promoting (or inhibiting) networking, but they cannot truly manage it. Observers often refer to networks when discussing administratively mandated arrangements, either within or between organizations, but such use of the term fails to capture the dynamism and vitality of true networking behavior.

Concepts from network analysis suggest two principles: (1) systematically planning and monitoring networking activities and (2) increasing network diversity.

Planning and Monitoring Networking Activities

Many divisions and barriers limiting the reach and diversity of networks are unplanned, institutionalized structures and processes that can be overcome with proper planning.

What Can Individuals Do?   Individuals, regardless of their organizational position, can enlarge their networks' reach by systematically charting their current networks and increasing their network-oriented behavior. A good place for individuals to begin is with an inventory of current ties, listing the people to whom they would go if they had a business problem and needed someone whom they could trust to give advice and support and to hold their conversation in confidence.

Next they should inventory their weak ties. Whereas they may have listed as few as four or five people under strong ties, their weak-ties relationships should be substantially larger. Entrepreneurs, for example, report that on the average they have spoken to nine or ten people for business advice in a six-month period (Aldrich, Reese, & Dubini, 1989). In an inventory, weak ties might be placed into categories by what resources or sources of information they represent.

People should then examine how active they have been in maintaining and expanding the circle of trust represented by people in their strong-ties network. When was the last time they saw them? How frequently have they seen them in the past year? Have they phoned them recently or sent a note?

As important as strong ties might be, weak ties are equally significant. How many lunch dates have they had in the past month with people they don't know personally but who are of value to their business (Welch, 1980)? Have they been seeing only people they know as friends? They might need to make a list of ideas on where and how they can meet those (unknown) people who are important to the success of their business.[3]

Networkers should put themselves in the path of important people by joining or attending meetings of trade and professional associations, civic groups, cultural institutions, charities, and other voluntary associations (Welch, 1980) and by making themselves visible within these organizations.

Finding people who play broker or bridging roles will allow someone to economize on the maintenance of their personal network, because such people substantially extend the reach of their network at the cost of maintaining only one more direct tie. They might find brokers by asking five or six people they know only casually (weak ties) to suggest someone with an expertise in the area with which they need help. It is not a good idea to ask their strong ties to suggest someone, as the reason for getting to know a broker well is to break out of one's personal network.[4]

What Can Managers Do?   Managers could look at all interorganizational transactions as opportunities to increase the level of networking by their employees. Many firms have reduced the size of their corporate research staff in response to increased competitive pressures, heightening the need for information from outside their boundaries. For example, during the 1980s, downsizing and reductions in hierarchical levels became the central theme of most U.S. Fortune 100 firms. These tactics systematically cut line and staff jobs dramatically, sometimes up to 25 percent. Such developments amplify a firm's need for increased external contacts to compensate for possible information deficits.

Thorelli (1986) viewed network management as a core function of managers, and although he was thinking primarily about interorganizational rather than interpersonal ties, his suggestions are well taken. He argued that managers should take a holistic view, integrating the various functional areas "both for internal effectiveness in serving other network members and for a unified approach to them." Adoutte (1989; 46–47) pointed out that high-technology firms, in pursuing a strategy of technology valorization, are looking for ways to generate new uses of their technologies. Working with other firms in exploring alternative uses for their technologies allows people to transcend the social boundaries that may have blinded them to hidden assumptions and implicit knowledge embedded in their current practices.

Consider a list of ways in which information and technology are shared among firms: licensing, joint ventures, turn-key operations, trade shows, direct sales, consultants, R&D consortia, cooperative alliances, hiring away each other's employees, and merger and acquisition activities. In many cases, these arrangements present managers with an opportunity to encourage their employees to engage in networking behavior. For example, most large Japanese and Korean trading companies devote substantial resources to tracking their business's interdependencies with other organizations (Auster, 1990). Within their industries, they show a high level of awareness of what other firms are doing. Many Japanese firms have their own in-house tracking and monitoring staff, and this function could be extended to maintaining records of their employees' significant business contacts. Only recently have U.S. firms begun to share research findings and information on new technologies via their participation in R&D consortia and as members of "best practices" company networks.

People in boundary-spanning roles of organizations play an important role in representing their organization to the outside, and in collecting and interpreting information for their organizations. Such people are often undervalued or even viewed with suspicion, and efforts may be made to routinize and formalize boundary roles to limit their discretion and power. If their activities are seen as including personal networking that may expand their organization's network linkages, managers may tolerate a higher level of ambiguity and discretion in such roles.

What Can Public Agencies and Consortia Do? Professional societies, workshop seminars, short-term consulting, and other activities that bring people face-to-face are repeatedly cited as the major ways in which technology is transferred. For example, Cutler (1989), in studying technology transfer in the United States and Japan, found that "researchers say they allocate the time they devote to exchanging new ideas as follows: Two-thirds is spent participating in talks, meetings, and working with leading colleagues; and one-third is spent reading, extracting, or preparing new information for publication or for patents" (74). For the fields of robotics, biotechnology, and ceramic materials, these conclusions were as true of the United States as they were of Japan. Personal contacts were the preferred ways for obtaining substantive information.

Cutler (1984) found that the Japanese had an advantage because Japanese companies had a more positive attitude about cooperative research, their researchers knew one another well because of an extensive network of academic and business committees, and personal commitment, trust, and desire for cooperation among researchers was high. Industrywide meetings made it possible for people in different companies to become familiar with new research, resulting in a rapid diffusion of ideas (Eager, 1985). Moreover, at these meetings, people who were familiar with work outside Japan acted as brokers and bridges, communicating their knowledge to people in different networks.

An example of an organization playing a broker role in the United States is the Marketing Sciences Institute (MSI), which is a private consortium of firms, each paying approximately $25,000 to belong. MSI focuses on improving research on marketing, and does this in part by promoting networking activities such as sponsoring conferences, running competitions, supporting research by academics through small grants, and distributing working papers.

Radosevic (1990) argued that small firms played an important role in technological development, in part through learning by interacting and by linking firms to one each other. He proposed the concept of a national system of learning, in which public agencies could encourage cooperative relationships between firms. In Japan, a branch of MITI—the Japanese External Trade Organization—tracks all forms of publicly announced linkages (Auster, 1990), and in Korea, KOTRA performs a similar function. In contrast, in the United States there is no centrally collected public information on the total spectrum of interorganizational linkages, although some information is available on joint ventures.

Public agencies and private planning bodies can create action sets— organizations formed for a specific purpose within a limited time frame by autonomous firms—and form new organizations that play broker roles, increasing network connections and information flow (Aldrich & Whetten, 1981). Since the National Cooperative Research Act was passed in 1984, more than 120 R&D consortia in the United States have formed (Evan & Olk, 1990).[5] Their characteristics are well known, and so we simply wish to point out that their success hinges in part on how successful they are at enlarging the personal networks of their participants (Rogers & Valente, 1991). For example, Admiral Bobby Ray Inman, Chairman and CEO of the Microelectronics and Computer Technology Corporation (MCC), planned that the managers who are in charge of their company's technology project would make frequent trips to the MCC. These monthly trips would bring the managers into contact with managers from other member companies, widening their weak-ties networks.

In Japan, the Small and Medium Enterprise Agency of MITI began encouraging the formation of Inter-Industrial Networks for Technological Activities [INTAC] about ten years ago, and in 1986 almost 1,000 networks were in existence (Furukawa, Teramoto, & Kanda, 1990). They are true action sets, composed of autonomous organizations, but many have evolved toward more formal structures.

INTACs are formed with flexible structures and stress personal interaction between members, such as meetings, visits, and so forth. Eventually, members share those resources that are mutually beneficial and supplementary. These networks lead to the sharing or acquisition of resources, which would not be possible through standard, arm's-length market mechanisms. Networks are allowed to evolve naturally, no administrative hierarchy actually puts people in touch with one another.

Action sets come in various guises, but all share a common characteristic: They concentrate and interpret information for their members. They make information more decision-relevant than the information obtained on the open market. Thus, people who play boundary-spanning roles—joining such organizations to outsiders—serve a significant networking function.

Increasing Network Diversity

A paradox of strong ties is that they provide strong socioemotional support for a person's activities while simultaneously limiting the diversity and chance encounters so essential for generation of new ideas. Expanding one's circle of weak ties is one way to increase diversity, but more direct measures are also needed.

What Can Individuals Do? The danger facing all business people is that the daily struggle to cope with pressing problems and keep up with expected routines gradually eliminates time spent in innovative activity (Mintzberg, 1974). People must set aside time for random activities—things done with no specific problem in mind. Cocktail parties, dinner engagements, get-togethers after work or on weekends, and other sociable occasions can lead to chance connections that increase the weak-ties network.

As a quick check on whether they may be sacrificing diversity for density in their personal network, people can take the list of people they generated for their strong-tie inventory and ask, "How many know one another?" The answer will probably be 50 percent or higher.[6] Then, people can do the same for their list of weak ties. If that answer is also 50 percent or higher, they may be involved in a network that is too in-grown and insulated to be of maximum benefit to them.

People can increase diversity in their network by consciously increasing the age range of people they know. For women, because the occupational distribution for younger women is significantly more like that for men than the distribution for older women, they can include younger women in their network. Younger women are likely to have the connections with men that older women need to overcome gaps in their own personal network because of gender barriers they may have previously encountered.

Assertiveness and an instrumental orientation pay off in building personal networks and are important in increasing network diversity. People should be self-promoting, not reluctant to explain to others how their product, service, or skills complement the other person's and thus establishing a common ground. When appropriate, follow-up meetings should be arranged with people who have something to offer. Finally, people can play broker roles themselves by bringing together people whose needs are complementary and can increase their visibility as brokers by taking credit for the results.

What Can Managers Do? In addition to the strategies we have listed to promote more networking, managers could also pay attention to the diversity of their firms' organization set—the set of all organizations to which they are directly connected (Aldrich & Whetten, 1981). The recruiting of new employees can be an occasion for increasing network diversity. In the past year or so, hundreds of Soviet mathematicians and physicists have emigrated to the United States, substantially affecting the thinking about many problems that had stumped American scientists for years. Although the Soviets were theoretical rather than applied scientists—their laboratory facilities tended to be inferior to those in the United States—they still brought fresh insights and ideas to the universities and businesses that hired them.

Managing diversity has become a new theme for many firms in the 1990s. By the year 2000, two-thirds of all new jobs will go to women, minorities, and immigrants. Failure to recognize work force diversity will result in decreased productivity and isolation of ethnic groups. Those companies that actively seek diversity, such as Proctor and Gamble, Hewlett-Packard, and Xerox, will capitalize in the benefits of a diverse work force. Numerous diversity awareness and training programs have emerged since Proctor and Gamble initiated its first in 1979. Two-thirds of all global migration is now to the United States, and thus U.S. managers must be proactive in encouraging diversity training in their domestic as well as in their international firms.

For multinational corporations (MNCs) operating abroad, hiring foreign nationals as managers has become a critical method for capturing and preserving local or implicit knowledge that can feed into an organization's internal network. Notwithstanding expatriate difficulties in assimilating into a new culture, this practice has gained in popularity in recent years. Even the Japanese have begun to place Americans in positions of power and authority in their U.S. operations. Mitsubishi practices this as "Americanization," and Nomura Securities, the world's largest securities firm, now has an American chairman.

Some firms keep their business units small and regionally oriented in recognition of the value of implicit knowledge. For example, ECCO, a leading French services company (human resources, safety, industrial cleaning, and banking and financial services), creates small operational units in various EEC countries that are run by small teams of local nationals who have also had one or two years of work experience in France. They have had an opportunity to experience culture clash, heightening their consciousness of the implicit knowledge of their own societies, which they bring to ECCO.

Some MNCs are setting up complementary R&D facilities in more than one country. "This strategy allows technological developments to be monitored, establishes communication links for technical flows across national boundaries, and establishes networks with universities and technical associations in other countries" (Keller & Chinta, 1990; 39). Keller and Chinta suggest that networking across firms and countries will be facilitated if companies place sophisticated technical personnel with a cosmopolitan orientation in boundary-spanning positions.

What Can Public Agencies and Consortia Do? Many of the strategies we have suggested for planning and monitoring networking can also affect the diversity of networks. For example, in Japan, membership in INTACs is limited to only one or two firms from the same industry. The purpose of this restriction is to limit the risk that business rivals will snatch away information and use it to their advantage, but it has the unintended consequence of making the INTACs more industrially diverse than they otherwise would be (Furukawa, Teramoto, & Kanda, 1990). Membership in the U.S. MSI is also deliberately spread across manufacturing, retail, and service industries to maximize the possibilities of cross-fertilization of ideas. Many U.S.-based consortia have published their "best practices," and these practices then are distributed across other networks.

In a technopolis, planners should deliberately create settings that facilitate face-to-face meetings between people from different organizations. Central meeting halls, recreation facilities, diverse cultural and entertainment activities, and many other tactics provide occasions for the chance encounters essential to broadening the reach and diversity of personal networks (Segal, 1988). Morita and Hiraoka (1988) noted that planners of the Osaka technopolis were concerned with preparing an alluring urban environment "with good housing and living conditions; a highly developed medical system; a favorable educational environment and opportunities; cultural, artistic, sports, and recreation facilities; and open-minded local communities. Such qualities will ensure the gathering of creative persons and the facilitation of face-to-face interchanges that are key factors in the creation of a successful technopolis" (38).

CONCLUSIONS

Recent political developments suggest we might be moving toward a world divided not by East versus West or North versus South but by regional trading blocs (Belous & Hartley, 1990): Europe, dominated by a united and prosperous Germany; Asia, dominated by Japan and the newly industrialized countries (NICs); and North America, dominated by the United States. The rest of the world will then be the last frontier of economic competition between these three spheres. Networks may be strongest within these three spheres, but they may be unable to penetrate very far into the others. Or some MNCs may develop networks that cut across regional boundaries, such as those occurring in the Maquiladoras, and therefore avoid being shut out. In the race for global competitiveness, networking will be an important strategy.

Individuals, firms, and public policy makers must pay more attention to systematically monitoring and planning networking and to increasing network diversity if they are to retain economic influence. Organizations of the future will be more self-conscious about networking—open information flow and diverse memberships, including partnerships and collaborative units, will expose organizations to more of their environments (Aldrich & Auster, 1987). In short, "boundaryless" organizations may dominate future organizational forms.

NOTES

1. Not all information is important. The information that businesses need most is rare, valuable, and inimitable (Barney, 1986). It must be rare, for otherwise, all businesses could obtain it and no competitive advantage could be gained. It must be valuable in the sense that it works. And, it must not be easily imitated or acquired by others or else it again loses its competitive advantage.

2. For example, when technology transfer is attempted, several problems involving implicit knowledge arise. First, the technology—at whatever level—may work as intended only when coupled with the tacit knowledge of the originating person, subunit, or organization. Second, the target organization or subunit may not be capable of absorbing, or even recognizing, the implicit knowledge needed to make the technology work.

3. For women, this list ought to specifically include cross-gender contacts (i.e., include men in positions of importance) to compensate for the high proportion of same-sex contacts most people make.

4. When you find a potential broker, take them out to lunch and pick up the tab. Follow the suggestions in Bixler (1984) regarding how to project a professional image when dealing with weak ties and potential brokers, who will not know others in your circle and thus have no preformed ideas about you.

5. Toshihiro Sasaki and Howard Aldrich are currently researching the longevity of the R&D consortia formed in the United States, and comparing their governance structures to those in Japan. Tentative results show that about one in seven R&D consortia have disbanded within the past five years.

6. In a study of the Research Triangle, density was about the same for men and women entrepreneurs: 55 percent for women and 58 percent for men (Aldrich, Reese, & Dubini, 1989). Similar findings have been obtained for Italy, Norway, and Sweden.

REFERENCES

Adoutte, R. "High Technology as a Commercial Asset." *International Journal of Technology Management,* vol. 4, 1989: 397–406.

Aldrich, H. E. & E. R. Auster. "Selezione Naturale E Strategia D'Impresa." *Sviluppo & Organizzazione,* no. 103 (Settembre-Ottobre), 1987:17–38.

Aldrich, H. E. & D. A. Whetten. "Making the Most of Simplicity: Organization Sets, Action Sets, and Networks." In P. Nystrom & W. Starbuck (Eds.), *Handbook of Organizational Design*. New York: Oxford, 1981:385–408.

Aldrich, H. E., P. R. Reese, & P. Dubini. "Women on the Verge of a Breakthrough?: Networking Among Entrepreneurs in the United States and Italy." *Entrepreneurship and Regional Development*, vol. 1, 1989:339–356.

Arrow, K. J. *The Rate and Direction of Inventive Activity: Economic and Social Factors*. NJ: Princeton Press, 1962.

Auster, E. R. "Task Characteristics as a Bridge between Macro- and Microlevel Research on Salary Inequality between Men and Women." *Academy of Management Review*, vol. 14, 1989:173–193.

Auster, E. R. "Bringing a Network Perspective into Research on Technological Transfers and Other Interorganizational Relations." In F. Williams & D. Gibson (Eds.), *Technological Transfer*. Newbury Park, CA: Sage, 1990.

Barney, J. "Organizational Culture: Can It be a Source of Sustained Competitive Advantage?" *Academy of Management Review*, vol. 11, 1986:656–665.

Belous, R. S. & R. S. Hartley (Eds.). *The Growth of Regional Trading Blocs in the Global Economy*. Washington, DC: National Planning Association, 1990.

Bixler, S. *The Professional Image*. New York: Putnam, 1984.

Cutler, R. S. "A Survey of High-Technology Transfer Practices in Japan and in the United States." *Interfaces*, vol. 19, no. 6 (November/December), 1989:67–77.

Eager, T. "Technology Transfer and Cooperative Research in Japan." *ONR Far East Scientific Bulletin*, vol. 10, no. 3, 1985:32–41.

Evan, W. & P. Olk. "R&D Consortia: A New U.S. Organizational Form." *Sloan Management Review* (Spring), 1990:37–46.

Fulk, J., E. M. Rogers, & M. A. von Glinow. "Diffusion of New Technologies in Third World Countries: A Comparison of Predictions from Three Alternative Theoretical Perspectives." *Organization and Change Management*, 1990.

Furukawa, K., Y. Teramoto, & M. Kanda. "Network Organization for Interfirm Research and Development Activities: Experiences of Japanese Small Businesses." *International Journal of Technology Management*, vol. 5, no. 1, 1990:27–40.

Gee, S. *Technology Transfer, Innovation, and International Competitiveness*. New York: Wiley, 1981.

Granovetter, M. "The Strength of Weak Ties." *American Journal of Sociology*, vol. 78 (May), 1973:1360–1380.

Granovetter, M. "The Strength of Weak Ties: A Network Theory Revisited." In Peter V. Marsden & Nan Lin (Eds.), *Social Structure and Network Analysis*. Beverly Hills, CA: Sage, 1982, pp. 105–130.

Hirschman, A. O. *Exit, Voice, and Loyalty*. Cambridge, MA: Harvard, 1972.

Kanter, R. *Men and Women of the Corporation.* New York: Basic Books, 1977.

Keller, R. T. & R. R. Chinta. "International Technology Transfer: Strategies for Success." *Academy of Management Executives*, vol. 4, no. 2 (May), 1990:33–43.

Kiechel, W. III. "Corporate Strategy for the 1990s." *Fortune*, vol. 117 (February 29), 1988:34–42.

Levin, D. P. "Motor City for Japanese in California." *New York Times,* May 7, 1990: C1–C2.

Maier, N. R. F. *Psychology in Industrial Organizations*, 4th edition. Boston: Houghton-Mifflin, 1973.

Millett, S. M. "The Strategic Management of Technological Research and Development: An Ideal Process for the 1990s." *International Journal of Technology Management*, vol. 5, no. 2, 1990:153–163.

Mintzberg, H. *The Nature of Managerial Work.* New York: Harper & Row, 1974.

Morita, K. & H. Hiraoka. "Technopolis Osaka: Integrating Urban Functions and Science." In R. W. Smilor, G. Kozmetsky, & D. V. Gibson (Eds.), *Creating the Technopolis: Linking Technology Commercialization and Economic Development.* Cambridge, MA: Ballinger, 1988: 23–50.

Radosevic, S. "The Role of Small Firms in Technological Development: An Interpretive Survey." *International Journal of Technology Management*, vol. 5, no. 1, 1990:89–99.

Rogers, E. M. & J. K. Larson. *Silicon Valley Fever: Growth of High-Technology Culture.* New York: Basic Books, 1984.

Rogers, E. M. & T. W. Valente. "Technology Transfer in High Technology Industries." In T. Agmon & Mary Ann Von Glinow (Eds.), *Technology Transfer in International Business.* Englewood Cliffs, NJ: Prentice Hall, 1991.

Segal, N. S. "The Cambridge Phenomenon: Universities, Research, and Local Economic Development in Great Britain." In R. W. Smilor, G. Kozmetsky, & D. V. Gibson (Eds.), *Creating the Technopolis: Linking Technology Commercialization and Economic Development.* Cambridge, MA: Ballinger, 1988:81–90.

Thomas, K. W. "Conflict and Conflict Management." In M. D. Dunnette (Ed.), *Handbook of Industrial and Organizational Psychology.* Chicago: Rand-McNally, 1976.

Thorelli, H. B. "Networks: Between Markets and Hierarchies" *Strategic Management Journal, vol. 7, 19*

Von Glinow, M. A., O. Schnepp, & A. Bhambri. "Assessing Success in US-China Technology Transfer." In T. Agmon & Mary Ann Von Glinow (Eds.), *Technology Transfer in International Business.* Englewood Cliffs, NJ: Prentice Hall, 1991.

Von Glinow, M. A. & M. B. Teagarden. *The Impact of Contextually Embedded Influences on Cooperative Alliance Performance: The Case of Sino-US*

Joint Ventures. Los Angeles, CA: University of Southern California, Graduate School of Business, 1990.

Welch, M. S. *Networking: The Great New Way for Women to Get Ahead.* New York: Harcourt Brace Jovanovich, 1980.

Williamson, O. "The Economics of Organization: The Transaction Cost Approach." *American Journal of Sociology*, vol. 87 (November), 1981:548–577.

13

Infrastructure for the Long Term via the Fine Grain

Stewart Brand

"Fast, cheap, and out of control," a slogan from the frontiers of artificial life research, characterizes the nature of adaptivity in communications-intensive technopolies. The technology environment is bound to remain turbulent and full of surprises so only fine-grained constant adaptivity can ensure sustainability over time. High-tech development flourishes best on a funky substrate.

With what images might we bracket that technopolis, Silicon Valley? The mythological but true image is of garages—the one in which Hewlett-Packard was founded in 1938 and the one in which Apple Computer was founded in the mid-1970s.

The most recent image—not mythic, merely true—is of spec office buildings. They dot the region. From a distance you can see right through them, nothing and no one in new, vacant rooms. Grass invades the empty parking lots. The building clings to hope for a couple of years. Then a window is broken and not repaired, and then the building becomes a forlorn hulk in a few months.

It's an instructive pair of images. The leading edge of technopolis is funky; the trailing edge is glitzy. If you get that backward and try to lead with glitz, you will get a funky trailing edge quickly, with no technopolis in between. You get Brasilia with fiber-optic cable—an expensive, embarrassing monument to over-reaching ambition. Big money, big ideas, and no life.

Remember "smart" office buildings? Ten years ago they were the future—densely wired sophisticated high rises designed to attract sophisticated communications-based companies. In Japan they worked somewhat, but in the United States and elsewhere they became no more than trade magazine cover stories. The tenants of the smart buildings, the few that came to those expensive spaces, blithely bypassed the communications systems and installed their own. To the building owners it was like seeing shanties go up in the broad streets of their

Brasilia. The tenants fought the buildings' centralized sensory and microclimate systems for a while and then began whining for windows that would just open. The fatal flaw here is overspecification.

Over-specified buildings became obsolete instantly because of cost and because they can't adapt. I remember the elaborately designed "Media Room" at MIT's Media Laboratory, where I once worked. With its rear-projection wall and advanced built-in stereo sound and complex wiring, it was state-of-the-art in 1985 when it was built with the rest of the $45 million Media Lab building, designed by I. M. Pei himself. The room was never used for media. Today it is a storeroom, and a poor storeroom at that. It is not part of the popular tours at the Media Lab.

What do garages and warehouses (the other popular start-up space) have in common? They're cheap and dry. No one cares what you do in them. So they are infinitely adaptable.

Recently I ran into John Sculley, President and CEO of Apple Computer, at a conference, and we began chatting about how his business constantly is expanding into more buildings. I asked if he preferred taking over old buildings or building new ones. He said, "Old buildings." I said, "Why?" And he said a curious thing, "Old buildings are more freeing."

BUSINESS LIFE: "ALWAYS ON THE EDGE OF CHAOS"

What's all this concern with adaptivity? I can't help it. I was originally trained as a biologist, and the first lesson of evolution is that inability to adapt in a turbulent environment is fatal. The current communications environment is highly turbulent and deeply unpredictable, yielding constant surprises, such as

- A little more than two years ago FAXes were a luxury for businesses. Last year they became a necessity. And despite the early bloom in Japan, neither the phone companies nor my futurist colleagues saw it coming.
- Cellular phones were supposed to fill a modest niche market. Some niche. They are redefining telephone systems.
- When backyard satellite dishes came out of the blue in the 1970s, none of the major electronic manufacturers were in the game. Three billion dollars of dishes were designed and manufactured by garage-based businesses.

The communications technology environment will not settle down in our lifetimes. There are many new frontiers that will be quickly self-rewarding and therefore will not wait for existing infrastructures to change. Some of the different, useful tools coming in the future are

- Electronic copresence, a term from researchers at Xerox PARC, who are demonstrating the usefulness of people working at a physical distance but in electronic intimacy over sustained periods of time. This usage will force more leased lines and more flat-rate pricing by telecommunications companies.

- Ubiquitous computing, also from PARC. With advances in microcellular technology will come an environment of intelligent devices in our work lives, all chatting merrily with each other. Your wristwatch and mine might argue about the time before they check with a local authority.
- Massive parallel processing, such as the already commercial Connection Machine. Dumb terminals will be gone, but your brilliant terminal may soon be praying for genius milliseconds from a remote massive parallel machine.
- Virtual reality—using eyephones and data suits for bodily immersion in computer-simulated worlds. Once this technology begins to flourish as a communication mediums—"shared dreaming" as Jaron Lanier calls it— then broadband will really take off.
- "Artificial life"—the focus of implosion of all the "connectionist" subdisciplines of computer science. These rich computer universes are inhabited with myriad diverse "agents" that learn and self-organize into ecosystems and economies.

Most of these technologies require and reward broadband communication, but when and how does that positive feedback begin, and how rapidly does it accelerate? We get glimpses. FAX is clearly an interim technology, but toward what and when?

In a turbulent communications environment, adaptivity wins, but what is the scale of adaptivity? Most adaptivity happens company by company, building by building, cable closet by cable closet, desk by desk—way below the purview of investors and planners of technopolies. Evolution is always and necessarily surprising. You cannot plan adaptivity or predict it; you can only make room for it—room at the bottom. Adaptivity is a fine-grained process. If you let it flourish, you get a wild ride, but you also get sustainability for the long term. You'll never be overspecified at the wrong scale. Mistakes will be small and disposable.

I suspect that the study of artificial life is going to change our ideas about organization, for it's so successfully bottom-up. You tweak the minute relationships among the educable agents, and you get emergent properties that startle you with their originality. Some of these systems can solve problems better than humans. We can predict that some of the slogans from the artificial life practitioners will migrate into human organization theory.

"The best things in life are grown." That piece of artificial life wisdom comes from Esther Dyson. (It reminds me of something her father, Freeman Dyson, said about engineering projects: "Quick is beautiful.")

The most popular artificial life slogan comes from Rodney Brooks, roboticist at MIT: "Fast, cheap, and out of control." Brooks makes robots that have their own minds; they flock like birds and do simple tasks, but there is no central control. He could unleash a horde of robots on the moon to prepare a moonbase just by ganging up and leveling moon turf. "Fast, cheap, and out of control" is not a bad description of living organisms.

Silicon Valley was originally envisioned by Frederick Terman, former Dean of Engineering at Stanford University, but it was not planned; it was grown out of scores of quick inexpensive projects. Once you get a local population of successful start-ups, then positive feedback and the companies increasingly gain by flocking together. After a certain window of potential competitivity has passed, other would-be Silicon Valleys have no chance; they are perpetually drained toward the real thing.

FOUNDING THE REAL THING

How would I start a technopolis? I'd look for technology with low threshold, infinite promise, and no special flocking. One such is nanotechnology—the convergence of a number of disciplines toward engineering on an infinitesimal, molecular scale. The domain doesn't exist yet, but it is highlighted in an excellent book, Drexler's *Engines of Creation*.

Then I'd look for the smartest, youngest people and ask them who and what they're interested in. I'd also look for a hungry, unobvious place with smart, ambitious people, a modicum of political and economic stability, and an interesting culture. South Africa and Italy come to mind. I'd connect that place electronically to the intellectual hotbeds of the world with a system designed to expand as need and opportunity suggest. And I'd look for existing, inexpensive space. The buildings of a defunct industry are ideal. I'd clear the way politically for new, inexpensive space—a low-tech/high-tech barrio with work and housing intermixed. If it's dense enough—twelve people or more per acre in the housing—then mass transit can work.

Recall the real history of Route 128 around Boston. When developers were selling those commercial properties, they showed in the promotional literature exactly how far the site was from the MIT campus.

Go to MIT and ask what is the most admired and productive building on that complex campus of gaudy structures. The most-loved and fertile place, the place of legend, is Building 20, the three-story wood radiation laboratory built as a temporary building back in 1942. To this day, more than fifty years later, it's the incubator for MIT's most inventive technologies and new disciplines.

A NOD TO THE COARSE GRAIN

Adaptivity and thus longevity is not only in the fine grain; it's also in the coarse grain—the domain larger than we usually think in. At the global business network we are exploring infrastructure problems, which are famously pandemic these days, as completely joined with environmental problems, also famously pandemic these days. In other words, if you think of environment as infrastructure, you get a valuable perspective on both; ideas from each can help solve the problems of the other. We've just begun to investigate the advantages of merging environment and infrastructure considerations, but I'll bet that the tools that emerge might help design more ecologically benign and inviting technopolies.

REFERENCES

Drexler, E. *Engines of Creation.* Garden City, NY: Doubleday, 1968.

14

Experiences and Plans for a EuroTechnopolis: EuroPark Alpha B1 in Mid-Germany

Gerhard O. Mensch

This chapter presents a case analysis of the EuroPark Alpha B1 project. Checkpoint Alpha is located where Highway B1 to Berlin crosses the border that once separated West and East Germany. As the iron curtain fell, the vision emerged to build a technology corridor, or even a science park, in mid-Germany with the possibility that it may grow into a technopolis. With "productivity shock" hitting former East Germany, unemployment and mass mobility may make this idea come true much faster than we had imagined.

The political and socioeconomic turbulences render projecting a planning and decision process under high uncertainty. This case analysis explains how the initiators try to cope with this uncertainty. The project may actually yield a high rate of return on equity at reduced levels of risk because of intranational and international support. In fact, building a global network of personal, institutional, technological, and financial supports is a precondition for success of the endeavor.

THREE DRIVING FORCES

Technopolis development can accelerate new technology-driven economic development in backward regions and can focus attention and concentrate resources for catching up. EuroPark Alpha B1 is targeted for implementing trend-setting infrastructures that will facilitate high-tech entrepreneurship in Germany, support effective commercialization into the European markets and beyond, and offer a life-enhancing environment.

The EuroPark concept evolved from experiences elsewhere in Europe, America, and Asia. In 1988–1989, our task force was involved in project design, city planning, architecture, and marketing development of an advanced science park in the Ruhr Valley. Earlier, we conceptualized the management structure and programs of the International Building Exhibition in Berlin. Alpha B1 is located in the middle between the two sites, which are two of the most populous industry centers in Europe. EuroPark Alpha B1 would actually constitute a link between the two that would eventually become a "technology corridor."

Plans are to develop the site gradually over several stages. However, events may pressure us to proceed more rapidly. Public funds are being offered to accelerate investment schedules. EuroPark Alpha B1 is expected to become a growthpole, which attracts people who desire a place that highlights creativity. EuroPark Alpha B1 is also expected to become a technical and social innovation; EuroPark Alpha B1 management strives for cultivating a distinctively pan-European flavor in the park's residential and commercial facilities.

Currently the two German states are going through extraordinary times. Legal, political, financial, social, and economic uncertainties abound. It is expected that East Germany will experience sustained growth. The good news is that this scenario is shared by economists and financial planners in the real estate industry. Triggered by market integration in western Europe and propelled by the sudden unification of the German markets, the prospects for return on property investments appear bright. However, there exists considerable short-term uncertainty concerning property rights and the use of real estate as collateral.

Nevertheless, the Old World hums of dynamism, liberalization and regulation in West European countries have accelerated cross-border traffic, exports, and imports and are likely to generate a wave of direct foreign investments in mid-Germany. The International Institute of Industrial Innovations recently finished a study on how corporate strategies cope with the new opportunities. To succeed in penetrating the European market, firms must use a unique selling proposition (USP), which has now become synonymous with unique selling presence. Firms from various countries are now looking for a location that is attractive for west European, north European, and North American company subsidiaries. EuroPark Alpha B1 will become an optimal industrial location for international firms who plan to serve the European market.

European countries have a more differentiated consumption pattern than, for example, North Americans. Hence, to be closer to the customer requires many European firms to diversify products and locations. EuroPark Alpha B1 addresses this need of international firms.

DEMAND PULL AND TECHNOLOGY PUSH

Within western and eastern Europe there exist considerable disparities in standard of living. According to a standard theory of foreign trade, these disparities will generate demand pull as those less well-off try to catch up. Figure 14.1 illustrates those disparities in terms of GNP per capita in 1989.

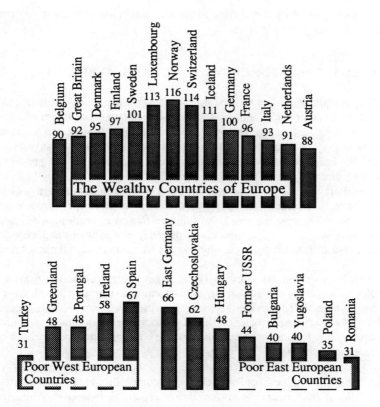

Figure 14.1. Europe's income differences in GNP in 1989.

Another factor that is likely to contribute to a take-off in mid-Germany soon is the current push of innovations. In many western countries, firms are near or at the cutting edge of modern technology. East German firms have missed out on most technological developments and now lag behind. However, in economic history we have seen that a country, once it shifts into gear to catch up with others, actually leapfrogs "best practice" and takes the technological lead.

The current wave of technological innovations in microelectronics, telecommunications, biotechnology, environmental protection, and energy offer new opportunities for lagging East European countries to improve productivity, repair horrendous environments (notably the former eastern Germany and Czechoslovakia), and replace unsafe infrastructures such as atomic reactors. In the former East Germany, deferred maintenance of houses, roads, railroads, bridges, plants, and equipment—for that matter, any capital stock—now generates excess demand for capital goods. Also, deferred demand for consumption goods adds to the inequilibrium. With the inflow of capital, capacity expansion can perhaps proceed at two-digit growth rates.

STRATEGY FOR LAUNCHING EUROPARK ALPHA B1

The EuroPark project will be promoted as an ethical investment program. "Ethical" means that it will address a vexing socioeconomic problem and generate social returns on investment that will probably amount to seven to ten times the private return on investment accruing to the initiators and private co-investors in the project. Nevertheless, it is expected that return on equity will be great because public subsidies will provide good leverage.

EuroPark Alpha B1 assesses the need of international high-technology companies to find suitable space in mid-Germany to serve the European market from that base. To serve that need, the standard two-stage real estate development process does not suffice. That process of property development and management would deliver a standard product, which is not what international clients need and want.

EuroPark Alpha B1 focuses on a target group of market-driven high-technology companies that need smart infrastructures to operate cost-effectively and need high value added services to succeed in the European market. Figure 14.2 exhibits how these need-oriented extras enrich the real estate on which the companies settle. Figure 14.2 also indicates that building global networks is viewed as an essential element for

1. Positioning the EuroPark relative to competing real estate, such that the EuroPark attracts the preferred user group (global networking enhances stature)
2. Providing the smart part of the infrastructure, namely, justification for installing the best design and capabilities at that time
3. Maintaining a sophisticated sales support service network that caters to the most ambitious and demanding performance requirements.

CASE ANALYSIS: TWO SOURCES OF
HIGH VALUE-ADDED SERVICES

Two main value-added sources in real estate development, science parks, and technopolies are knowledge and capital. This is easily stated but difficult to implement, if the joint output of the two inputs is the end result of a multistage process of development.

In our planning we distinguish the capital-intensive path and the research-intensive path (Figure 14.3). Capital intensive means that the initiator starts with a mountain of capital and catches knowledge as it comes and is needed. Research

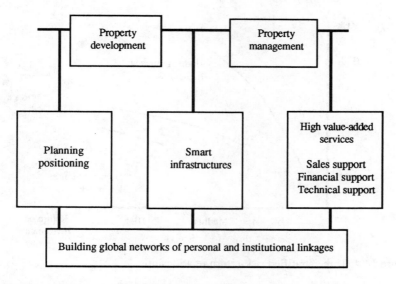

Figure 14.2. The three-layer real estate development process.

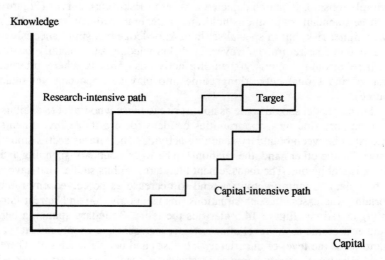

Figure 14.3. Capital-intensive and research-intensive paths in real estate development.

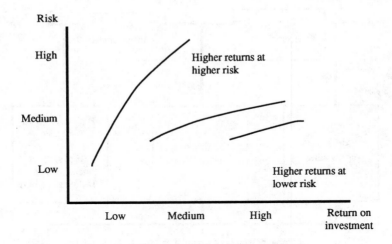

Figure 14.4. Three stratified risk-return relationships.

intensive means spending a large fraction of one's total effort on learning and later raising funds as becomes necessary. The EuroPark developers follow the latter path because it provides a higher return on equity and better leverage on sweat capital.

In the research-intensive approach, knowledge generates a stratified risk-return relationship. It can be depicted as a set of risk-return curves (Figure 14.4). The three financial propositions hold that in general, you can have higher return only at higher risk, but in special settings, knowledge can simultaneously reduce risk and increase return. However, such knowledge must usually be sourced elsewhere through boundary-spanning activities. This is where international exchange and global networking come into play as important yet intangible resources.

Such a model should come as no surprise to those who travel to exhibits often and commonly find new opportunities or ideas for profitable investments. The relationship between boundary-spanning activities and returns seems smooth and positive. On the other hand, the relationship between boundary-spanning activities and risk is ambiguous. The management literature exhibits studies that have shown that boundary-spanning activities tend to decrease as perceived environmental uncertainty increases. In such situations, managers give up and retreat into their own organizations. Figure 14.5 clarifies the issue. Boundary-spanning behavior can either decrease as the level of uncertainty increases and people retreat for cover or increase as the level of uncertainty increases and people reach out. There exist trade-offs between staying home and traveling abroad when uncertainties exist. In the development of EuroPark Alpha B1, the link between global networking and reduced risk appears positive and strong. In this case, building a global network will probably pay off.

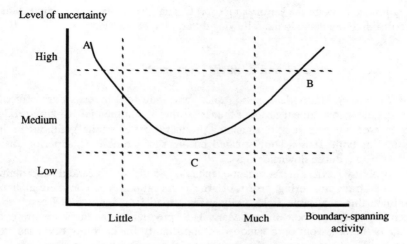

Figure 14.5. Global networking activity level depends on level of perceived uncertainty.

CONCLUSION

It is often asked if the time and cost spent on travel, the preparation time away, and follow-up make sense. From a strategic management point of view, global networking is a condition *sine qua non* in cases such as EuroPark Alpha B1. Boundary-spanning travel eases the planning process; helps position the project; and facilitates the inclusion of soft items (intangibles) into the budget, notably expenses for intelligent infrastructures and sophisticated services that appear to be the most productive factors in reducing the business risks of the venture and increasing the prospective yield of the entire enterprise.

APPENDIX A

Summary of the European Export Capital Fund

An important part of this case analysis is the financial engineering design of the building program, including equipping the EuroPark with intelligent infrastructures on the one hand, and the marketing program, including bringing a network of sophisticated services, on the other. The second task is being accomplished by a combination of supply and demand; namely, the developers of EuroPark Alpha B1 partly supply such services according to plan and partly supply them on demand from clients that purchase those services in combination with being funded through the European Export Capital (EEC) Assurance Fund. This is described in more detail in the following description of the fund.

EEC Assurance Fund Limited Partnership

Summary. Individual, institutional, and industrial investors are offered a new specialty investment product that is neither a commercial-banking product (export credits) nor a venture-financing product (start-up capital), although it has features of both. It is a sophisticated buy-in fund combining superior upside choices with reduced downside risks.

Mobility barriers in transatlantic technology trade offer splendid opportunities for generating pioneering profits. Large corporations and commercial banks dominate this profitable field. Only a few small-firm innovations reach their potential foreign-market niches. Many U.S. product innovations are life-cycle products that miss out on a window of opportunity for doubling revenues from exports to Europe, an opportunity that often yields triple returns on sales.

However, to capture these extra gains, timing and cost-effective entry is crucial. This is *terra incognita* for most organizations in the conventional export services field. This is where the fund comes in.

Many small U.S. companies have been formed recently around leading-edge products that after having become best-sellers in U.S. market niches might sell equally well in European countries if only some mobility barriers could be removed. The EEC Assurance Fund provides a new capital market instrument for helping these American firms as they begin to enter or expand in the European market.

The fund is a financial innovation and a marketing innovation aimed at superior gains in international commercialization of new high-technology products and services. The General Partners have tried to implement the motto of Rod Canion, CEO and Founder of Compaq Computer Corporation, which grew from zero sales in 1982 to more than $2 billion in 1988. During its rapid growth, Compaq learned some lessons about running a technology-based business in today's intensively competitive marketing environment. The most important was the fact that bringing high technology to the marketplace requires more innovations in business and marketing methods than it does in technology. The managing and marketing methodology implemented in design and operations of the fund works best in "Trans-Atlan-Tech-Trade." Trans-Atlan-Tech-Trade is a trademark of Mensch & Partners, a financial engineering consultancy firm affiliated with the General Partners in the fund.

Actually, the EEC Fund aspires to superior returns at reduced uncertainty, owing to its unique approach at providing its target group of investees (i.e., young, dynamic U.S. innovation companies on advanced levels of commercialization) with an intelligent infrastructure and sophisticated market penetration services. The EEC Fund implements an innovative, two-pronged approach that maximizes return on sales on American innovations in European exports through the use of intelligent infrastructures at science parks and technology centers cooperating with the fund, notably the EuroPark AlphaB1 in mid-Germany, and through the cultivation of sophisticated sales support services designed for high-market performance. This approach is carried out by a value-added network of business units.

The General Partners' general partner, 3IN Investment in Innovation Ltd., Inc., in Cambridge, Massachusetts, is a member of the IN-Group, a proprietary network of fund management companies, consultancy partnerships, and the 4IN International Institute of Industrial Innovations, Cambridge and Munich, one of the leading innovations research houses in America and Europe. Recently, 4IN Europe performed under contract from the European Commission an industry study on the emerging European information services market for infoproducts and databases that serve consortia of high-technology investors.

4IN is a leading provider of due diligence work (technology assessments and market assessments). 3IN and 4IN have sometimes helped U.S. firms enter the European market, assisted by Mensch 3IN Europe GmbH and by Mensch & Partners, one of several top management consultancies in Europe that have formed the Association of International Consultancies (AIC). As an example of recent achievements, AIC/Mensch & Partners have provided, under contract with the State of Northrhein Westfalia and the Ruhr Valley Authorities, the development plan and the marketing concept for the Ruhr Valley Science Park and Technology Centers.

The European operations of the EEC Fund will be managed by Mensch 3IN Europe GmbH, Munich. The management company will be assisted by AIC and by Mensch & Partners. Mensch & Partners and Mensch 3IN Europa GmbH also serve the EuroPark Alpha B1 consortium, which develops and builds that facility as project managers and consultants. The Mensch business units guide the implementation of the intelligent infrastructures and sophisticated sales support services to maximize returns on sales of American product innovations marketed in Europe by subsidiaries or joint venture companies based in EuroPark Alpha B1.

Investment Strategy. Key factors of success are access to a large pool of new products that in their U.S. market have succeeded in reaching an advanced stage of market penetration while still new to Europe, and the ability to select potential "winners" and support them to win. Both factors are in place. 3IN USA is a coinvestor in one of the largest American programs of syndicated coinvestments in new product innovations. Also, through its due diligence work and its cutting-edge innovations research, 4IN USA has hundreds of leads for prospective users of our European infrastructures and service network. For example, 4IN USA is currently ploughing through about 1,000 files on recent U.S. innovations to determine market share dynamics and profit performance of 150 pioneering firms. The task is to analyze a representative sample of innovations. This work, done under contract from the U.S. Small Business Administration, illustrates the scope of our capabilities to contact prospects, select them according to the fund's mission, generate deal flow cost-effectively, and control subsequent performance in Europe.

The competitive advantage of the EEC Fund is in the target area of Trans-Atlan-Tech-Trade of small high-tech firms, where banks tend to be relatively absent or narrow in support capability.

The fund reduces the technological risk in the portfolio by selecting new technologies that have performed well for some years in the U.S. market. On the production side, initial flaws have all been eliminated and economies of scale have been achieved. A subsidiary of 3IN, the 4IN International Institute of Industrial Innovations, Cambridge/Munich, is monitoring the candidate technologies and potential rivals. The market and management risks in new-technology exporting are reduced by providing portfolio companies with the best market research, management consulting, and information services in Europe, at EuroPark Alpha B1 in mid-Germany, and other connected sites.

The main determinant of success is cost-effectiveness in European sales operations. The weakest link in the export business of small technology companies always has been and continues to be trustworthy supervisory capacity. For the individual firm, it is too costly as an overhead item. This is where the real advantage of the EEC Fund approach will come to fruition: combining a hands-on approach with remote control that is disciplined by the General Partners' self-interest in maximizing returns on sales in companies backed with the fund's resources. One aspect of value-added services is overhead economy. The most important aspect, however, which is often overlooked in the high-technology exporting business, is opportunity cost economy. Many remote-controlled foreign units of small U.S. technology firms tend to perform far below potential. They bring home only a minor fraction of potential revenues and earnings. The EEC Fund's operative management concentrates on harnessing these two sources of value.

15

Information and Communications Technology: A Strategic Choice of the Italian Technopolis

Umberto Bozzo

Tecnopolis Novus Ortus, shortly named Tecnopolis,[1] is the first Italian experience in setting up an intensive knowledge site to provide start-up aid for attracting advanced or high-technology firms and for building or expanding indigenous companies. By the early 1980s, southern Italy ("Mezzogiorno"), as well as other structurally weak areas in the European community,[2] showed a growing tendency to become cut off from the new economic development induced from the renewal of manufacturing in the highly industrialized regions in Europe. Italy's regional gap is a matter of debate; after forty years of "special intervention," the Mezzogiorno has achieved a per capita income that is 59 percent of the national average (rather less than it was in the 1970s) and has a 21 percent rate of unemployment (more than three times that of the north), of which more than 40 percent is under the age of 25.[3]

Major companies and their R&D divisions have tended to become concentrated in certain central areas or agglomerations, where the technology development capacity was more suitable to the latest economic trends (Higgins et al., 1988; Goddard et al., 1988). A smaller share for the labor element in value creation, more product and process innovations, new factors affecting location, and migration of skilled labor to central areas have been the main effects of the peripheral and central regions' economic game as opportunities for defining and implementing its mission by the Centro Studi Applicazioni in Tecnologie Avanzate (CSATA), a research consortium promoted by the University of Bari.

In 1984, CSATA started the technopolis experience as a proactive strategy for the creation of suitable conditions for the realization of technological progress as a framework for economic development. The future success of the technopolis over the next ten to fifteen years will be contingent on the following factors:

- The relatively good image of the social and economic conditions of the Apulia region and of its capital Bari
- The good reputation of the University of Bari
- Policy, both at state and at European Community levels, which is oriented to fostering and managing economic growth and technological innovation
- The capacity of CSATA in the new information technology field after fifteen years of work.

INFORMATION TECHNOLOGY AND TECHNOPOLIS DEVELOPMENT

The demand for information and communication technology derives from a growing demand for information. Great attention has been focused on the new flexible location of organizations made possible by telecommunications and on the basic conditions for realizing long-term and irreversible economic implications of the technological process. Therefore, as a framework to the development of technopolis as a human and technology site where the companies meet their information needs, the basic orientation has been taken from the definition of information economy summarized in the following statements (Goddard & Gillespie, 1986; Hepworth, 1989; Monk, 1989):

- Knowledge, expressed in information that can be exchanged, processed, transferred, and applied, plays a large role in the effective production and delivery of goods and services in all sectors of the world economy.
- Economic change induced by the large role of information is supported by the changes through which information travels and can be used with computer networking as a key spatial component in the technical infrastructure of the information economy.
- The tradeable information sector in the economy is growing with the inclusion of traditional information activities such as the media and advertising and the creation of new industries such as on-line information services.
- The growth of the advanced producer service sector can in part be accounted for by the externalization of information functions from manufacturing and other firms.
- The growing "informatization" of the economy is making possible the global integration of national and regional economies.

As a consequence of this perspective, the first stage of technopolis development has the following objectives:

- To design and to implement a technological infrastructure, based on advanced telecommunications and computing facilities as a location factor for large companies and as a linkage to the world for the small or start-up companies (Blakely et al., 1987; Malecki, 1988)

- To promote new activities (the creation of data banks and wide national and international interest) and the brokering of on-line information services
- To propose to existing companies the externalization of information functions (such as technical writing, technical language translation, electronic publishing, computer-aided design of electronic components, and software production)
- To assess the conditions for the evolution of the new activities and of the externalization of information functions into new small enterprises to be located in the technopolis
- To set up joint research projects with large companies interested in the location of their own R&D facilities in the technopolis. This would facilitate the access to the advanced labor skills and equipment of CSATA and to professors and students from the University of Bari.

To overcome the peripherality of the region, from a geographical and socioeconomic point of view, the activities for the first-stage implementation of the technopolis program have been put in the framework of European programs. After the opening of its first facilities in 1984 on a 90-acre core area, the technopolis constituted six buildings with 200,000 square feet, with two more buildings under construction (an additional 150,000 square feet). The two new buildings have been completed and support new and early-stage advanced technology enterprises in an incubator and host cooperative research projects with large companies in a multitenant facility. Continued growth is expected to expand the core technopolis population to more than 750 people by 1993.

The major areas of growth are information and communication technology, microelectronics, and laser technology. New prospect areas are factory automation, space, and medical instruments. Eleven companies and other organizations are located in the technopolis, three have announced plans to locate there, and ten are implementing a location feasibility analysis. Four hundred scientists, engineers, technicians, and support staff are working in the technopolis. The R&D facilities of three large companies have moved from their headquarters' core area to the 800-person R&D sites linked to the technopolis.

TECHNOPOLIS-RELATED EUROPEAN COMMUNITY PROGRAMS

Telecommunications, computing, and broadcasting technologies are merging, and the roles of the public and private sectors are being reappraised.[4,5] The introduction of the Integrated Services Digital Network (ISDN) will facilitate the integration of speech, data, and picture transmission in a single network. Based on the concept of open-system interconnection (OSI), the ISDN will allow the use of the same terminals and standardized services across national frontiers.

By the end of 1992, 80 percent of European community subscribers should be within reach of an ISDN-capable exchange. The evolution of ISDN into an open-network infrastructure for Europe will enable the provision of services to develop according to user demand. The development of ISDN, making full use of the existing local networks, will be followed by the introduction of general broadband communication based on fiber-optics, providing the means for the convergence of telematics and the audiovisual sector into the integrated broadband communication (IBC) by 1995.

The value-added services, identified as an essential part of the information-based economy, including nonvoice services (EDP time-sharing and database services; videotex services, electronic data interchange within industries, and mailbox and message handling) and telephone services (conference calls and telephone message services), are experimented with and promoted at regional levels using existing communications infrastructures and exploiting the results of research activities. Criteria for selecting projects and appropriations for priorities have been derived in the technopolis from European Community plans of action for R&D in advanced communications technology (RACE), for improving the supply of advanced telecommunications services (STAR), and for setting up an information services market (IMPACT).

INFORMATION AND COMMUNICATION TECHNOLOGY INFRASTRUCTURE

The key issue of the strategy in developing the technological capacity of the technopolis is the qualification of the site as a communications pole in the national and international networks, integrating and connecting at different geographical sites (local, metropolitan, and regional) the academic and industrial research infrastructure, the technological innovation diffusion infrastructure, and the manufacturing and service sectors. The strategy is based on the following factors:

- Integrating of network systems at transport and management levels
- Interworking of heterogeneous networks supporting the portability and the cooperation of services in different network environments
- Complying with national and international communications standards
- Upgrading the different networks and services in agreement with service providers and users.

The primary poles of different networks, such as GARR, IATINET, and regional and local networks, are located in the technopolis.

The GARR Network

At the end of 1988, the Italian Minister of Universities and Scientific and Technological Research founded the commission Gruppo Armonizzazione delle Reti per la Ricerca—Group for the Harmonization of Networks for Research (GARR). The GARR Commission, where the technopolis is one of the eight national representatives, as a national reference point for computer interconnection projects for scientific research, sets up a common plan for migration toward ISO/OSI standards, and promotes a unified participation of Italian organizations to international associations and projects.

The GARR Commission has been the main coordinating body for the drafting and creation of the project "High-Speed Network Infrastructure for Italian Research" (Figure 15.1). The architecture of the backbone is made up of 2 Mbps data transmission lines and multiplexors, used for four communication architectures (SNA, DECNET, X.25, and TCP/IP) awaiting migration to ISO/OSI standards. The GARR network is connected to the following international networks:

- High-Energy Physics Network (HEPNET/SPAN)
- European Academic Research Network (EARN/Bitnet)
- INTERNET/NSFNET (TCP/IP Academic Network in USA)
- European Academic Supercomputing Initiative Network (EASINET)
- International X.25 Infrastructure (IXI), an X.25 European network backbone promoted by COSINE.

IATINET Network

The IATINET network is the main communication infrastructure for southern Italy (Figure 15.1). This network connects all the research centers in southern Italy. The technopolis is the gateway between the GARR and IATINET networks. The IATINET network will be integrated with two Eutelsat I satellite networks for videoconferencing (2 Mbps) and for data transmission (128 Kps). Through these satellite networks, traveling units will support demo and education activities in many southern Italy regional areas.

Regional and Metropolitan Networks

Universities, national research organizations, and many industrial areas and local government offices are connected through public and private data networks to technopolis (Figure 15.2 and Figure 15.3). A metropolitan area network (MAN) based on fiber-optic technology is being established in the frame of a joint project with the public provider SIP. The MAN is connecting technopolis to its local users basin and constitutes a suitable infrastructure for the experimentation of broadband network services and for high-speed LAN-to-LAN connections.

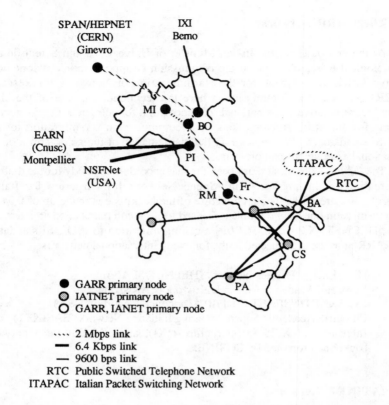

SPAN/HEPNET
(CERN)
Ginevro

IXI
Bemo

MI

BO

EARN
(Cnusc)
Montpellier

PI

NSFNet
(USA)

ITAPAC

RTC

Fr

RM

BA

CS

PA

● GARR primary node
◉ IATNET primary node
○ GARR, IANET primary node

···· 2 Mbps link
— 6.4 Kbps link
— 9600 bps link
RTC   Public Switched Telephone Network
ITAPAC Italian Packet Switching Network

Figure 15.1. Technopolis hostnode of international and national networks.

Technopolis Communication and Computing Node

As shown in Figure 15.4, the technopolis's laboratories constitute a complex, heterogeneous computing environment whose facilities are accessible through an on-site LAN. The availability of multivendor equipment is a key issue in the technopolis, as it is intended to grant state-of-the-art technology in each competence domain.

From their workstations, local and remote users can easily benefit from the availability of integrated software environments supporting many applications. Specific attention is paid by the technopolis to the problems of physical and logical interpretation of the several network infrastructures. Network interworking is operated by bridges and gateways at different levels, ranging from physical to service levels, thus favoring an easy and transparent access to the resources attached to any network infrastructure. In this sense, the migration processes to OSI standards are furthered.

Figure 15.2. Technopolis regional network.

MAIN ACTIVITIES BASED ON INFORMATION
AND TELECOMMUNICATIONS TECHNOLOGY

The information and communication technology infrastructure is the layer on which the other three types of complementary and integrated infrastructures (education and training, transfer and diffusion, and R&D) are in the implementation and experimentation stages. These infrastructures are designed to achieve technological change objectives and to promote specific types of investment for a total capital growth (physical capital plus human capital plus capital knowledge) (Kozmetsky, 1987; Capron, 1988).

The three infrastructures must fulfill the conditions for a public-private development strategy aimed to:

- Develop a capacity for technological assimilation by intensive investments in education and job training (education and training infrastructure)
- Promote a capacity for technological adaptation by favoring purchase of patents, licenses from abroad, and technical assistance (technology diffusion infrastructure)
- Sustain a capacity for technological advancement by financing specific R&D projects (R&D infrastructure)
- Create a socioeconomic environment favorable to technological development, one important determinant of long-run growth and international specialization (Commission of the European Communities, 1989; Porter, 1990).

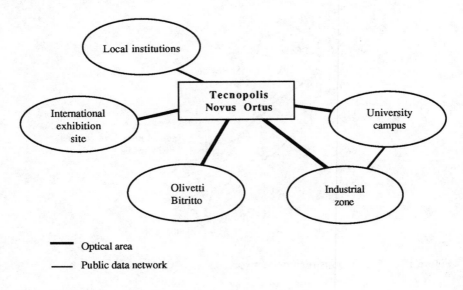

Figure 15.3. Technopolis metropolitan network.

EDUCATION AND TRAINING

An important element of technopolis development is the training program, which provides a steady flow of qualified people to the existing companies. Experts for the supply sector and trained users for the demand sector are equipped with the necessary skills and knowledge through applied multidisciplinary work and intensive use of all available technological facilities for making high-level contributions to the information market growth in the region. About forty post-doctoral students, fifty experts and four hundred users every year are trained to support high-level technopolis activity.

Besides educational and training activities concerning technology transfer in the technopolis, two more programs are emphasized in the education infrastructure. These programs promote the awareness of innovation as a cultural component of the people living, studying, and working in the area and stimulate the interest for new business formation and good business administration. Students and teachers from secondary schools, civil servants, workers in companies, and journalists visit the technopolis throughout the year. During these visits, professors and students, managers and technical staffs, entrepreneurs interested in diversification, and young people in general are invited to start new business projects.

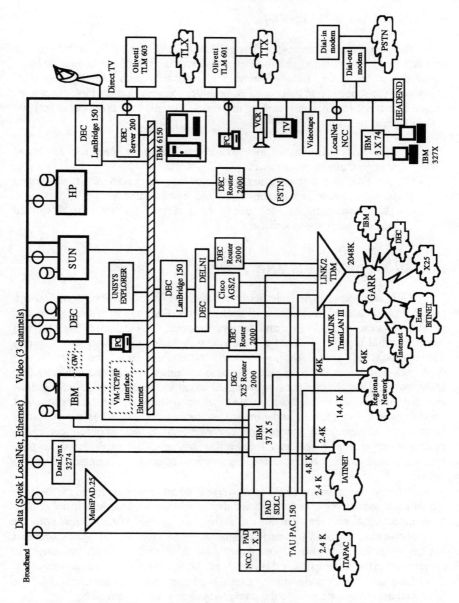

Figure 15.4. Technopolis communication and computing infrastructure.

TECHNOLOGY DIFFUSION

The purpose of technology diffusion (Bozzo & Gibson, 1990) in informatics and communications is to contribute to the strengthening of the economic base, foster job creation, and raise technological standards in the Apulia region by improving the supply of advanced telecommunications services and integrating the region into large telecommunications networks. Broadly, the program covers the following operations:

- The establishment of the basic equipment needed for advanced telecommunications services
- The establishment and development of laboratories to quality check and measure telecommunications electronic digital components
- The promotion of the supply of and the demand for advanced telecommunications services.

R&D IN INFORMATICS AND TELEMATICS AREAS

R&D activities in the technopolis are focused on evaluation, development, and application of information (and telematics) technologies in such strategic sectors as microelectronics, robotics and factory automation, land management, and environmental protection. Joint applied research projects are carried out among Tecnopolis CSATA and leading industrial companies interested in the direct exploitation of the results. R&D activities also are aimed at developing the required know-how and capabilities for supporting diffusion and technology transfer actions and for promoting and attracting production initiatives. In fact, industrial partnerships are conceived and pursued at the research stage as the basis for favoring the settlement of joint or independent initiatives, which in turn can create reference structures in the area for the development and exploitation of new technologies, thus contributing to the improvement of the local demand and supply system.

A further contribution to the improvement of this system is given through the provision of testing services for both standard conformance assessment and quality assurance. Such services are aimed at improving the qualification and the competitiveness of local and national producers in view of the open European market in 1993. A testing laboratory for information technology products is operational in the technopolis and is mainly active in communications products.

Current activity programs in distributed systems and applications in the advanced networks field refer to the market scenario as characterized by

- The diffusion of heterogeneous information systems that are required to interwork

- The evolution toward integrated digital telecommunication technologies and facilities (B-ISDN, IBCN, high-speed local and metropolitan networks)
- The growing need for multimedia information integration for applications in office automation, teleeducation, and other industrial activities.

As a whole these programs are characterized as dealing with

- Design and development of distributed applications across interconnected heterogeneous systems conforming to the current reference models and standards (e.g., ISO/OSI) or contributing to their development (this is also pursued through direct participation in standards working groups)
- Prototyping software environments for supporting distributed applications and integrating multimedia distributed databases
- Presentation, handling, and storing of multimedia documents on advanced workstations
- Promotion and experimentation of new applications and services for specialized user communities (e.g., interpersonal message systems and their connections; directory services; electronic data interchange for office applications; and e-mail systems management tools and services in distributed multimedia environments).

In the perspective of accessing anticipated IBC networks, a multiannual R&D program concerns the design, development and experimentation with the functions of an advanced, low-cost, multimedia workstation for supporting office, interactive teleeducation, and other industrial applications. Investigations and developments are carried out on representation formats of multimedia documents (with reference to international standards) on techniques and tools for their acquisition, processing, storing, transfer, and restitution on user-friendly human interfaces. In the frame of the technopolis optical basin initiative, experimental televideomatic services will be set up and provided. Accordingly, broadband communications technology and services are currently under investigation and development at the technopolis and its partners' premises; studies and developments are related to innovative service design and implementation, multimedia information storing and transfer, presentation and processing technologies, and interconnection to outerterrestrial and satellite-based networks.

TECHNOPOLIS AND ITS FUTURE

Technopolis development is dynamically driven by a continuous monitoring. This monitoring qualifies both the new physical and technological investments and the upcoming education, training and diffusion, technology transfer, and R&D activities.

But above all, the relationships among institutional organizations (industry, university, local authorities, and financial institutions) take part in the implementation of the technopolis in the awareness that the intelligence and culture of the people who represent these institutions will determine the real integration of the technopolis into the worldwide network of new human and technology sites.

NOTES

1. Centro Studi Applicazioni in Tecnologie Avanzate (CSATA) is the name of the consortium created in 1969 by the University of Bari that originated the idea of a technopolis, a property-based initiative that has links with universities and research centers and promotes local socioeconomic development through technology transfer, in southern Italy. Tecnopolis Novus Ortus is the name of the technopolis created by CSATA and a trademark registered in 1984. Tecnopolis CSATA Novus Ortus is the name of CSATA since 1988, and it clearly identifies the consortium in charge of running the first Italian technopolis. Novus Ortus is the Latin translation of the word "renaissance."

2. European parliament, Directorate-General for Research, Background Document on Science and Technology Parks, 1989.

3. *Financial Times Survey.* Italy, April 17, 1990.

4. Commission of the European Communities Green Paper on the development of the common market for telecommunications services and equipment. Report on the state of implementation. Brussels and Luxembourg, 1989.

5. Commission of the European Communities guidelines for improving the synergy between the public and private sectors in the information market. Brussels and Luxembourg, 1989.

REFERENCES

Blakely, E. J., B. H. Roberts, & P. Manidis. "Inducing High-Tech: Principles of Designing Support Systems for the Formation and Attraction of Advanced Technology Firms," *International Journal of Technology Management*, vol. 2, nos. 3/4, 1987.

Bozzo, U. & D. V. Gibson. "The European Experience: Technology Transfer Prospects for 1992." In F. Williams & D. Gibson (Eds.), *Technology Transfer: A Communication Perspective.* Newbury Park, CA: Sage Publications, 1990.

Capron, H., "Towards Global Microeconomic Models with Technological Change." In *Technology Management I.* New York: Interscience Enterprises Ltd., 1988.

Commission of the European Communities. *European Competitiveness in the 21st Century: Integration of Work, Culture and Technology.* Brussels: FAST Program CEC, June 1989.

Goddard, J., D. Charles, J. Howells, & A. Twaithes. *Research and Technological Development in the Less Favoured Regions of the Community.* Brussels, CEC, 1988.

Goddard, J. B. & A. E. Gillespie. "Advanced Telecommunications and Regional Economic Development." *Geographical Journal*, vol. 152, no. 3, 1986.

Hepworth, M. E. *Geography of the Information Economy.* London: Belhaven Press, 1989.

Higgins, T., C. Maguire, & S. Nielsen. *Science and Technology for Regional Innovation and Development.* Luxembourg: CEC, 1988.

Kozmetsky, G. "Economic Growth through Technology: A New Framework for Technology Commercialization in Economic Development Alliances," In G. Kozmetsky, R. W. Smilor, & E. Chamberlain (Eds.), *Economic Development Alliances.* Austin, TX: IC^2 Institute, The University of Texas at Austin, 1987.

Malecki, E. J. "Technical Workers and the Location of R&D Facilities," *Technology Management I.* New York: Interscience Enterprises Ltd., 1988.

Monk, P. *Technological Change in the Information Economy.* London: Pinter Publishers, 1989.

Porter, M. E. "The Competitive Advantage of Nations," *Harvard Business Review.* (March-April), 1990.

Part Five

Strategic Alliances for Development:
Ways to Facilitate Cooperation among
Multiple Companies and Countries

16

Economic Development, Technology Transfer, and Venture Financing in the Global Economy

Richard W. Morris

In a recent article, Harold Malmgren (1990) calls attention to the impact of technological advances on government and industry:

> Technological advances are now well under way, and cost advantages of their applications are giving rise to major structural adjustments in all national economies, and are causing substantial shifts in the pattern of world movement of goods, services and capital.
>
> Technological advancements are bringing about profound changes in the organization of work, of governance, and of social life." (Brock & Hormats, 1990; 93)

Warning of their potentially overpowering effects on governments and national economies, Malmgren states that these advances are proceeding faster than the capacity of our societal institutions to adapt to their consequences. He suggests a requirement for new institutions and adaptive mechanisms and thereby places the nature of our future global economy in the realm of the technopolis and smart infrastructure. With these issues in mind, this essay will review those economic, geopolitical, and technological forces that are currently shaping the emerging technopolis industry and will discuss one example of an organization that is seeking to respond constructively to these forces on behalf of the inhabitants and institutions in its surrounding region.

To venture a working definition, the technopolis industry is comprised of concepts, institutions, programs, policies, structures, and strategies that exploit advanced technologies for the development of efficient urban forms. Functionally, the technopolis is developed according to all or some of the following criteria:

- Incorporates technological advances in basic infrastructure and utilities
- Comprises institutions and resources that hasten the application and diffusion of technological innovation
- Enhances or protects the quality of life and overall human condition
- Links the inhabitants of the technopolis globally for the widest possible range of forms of communication and transaction.

Today, global conditions influence each function, while creating unique needs and opportunities that will determine the future of the technopolis. As a case in point, I suggest that the programs proposed for development at the Texas Research and Technology Foundation (San Antonio) are a useful and transferable model for the successful technopolis.

GLOBAL TRENDS

At least nine economic and geopolitical trends are influencing the way that we run governments and do business in the world today (Figure 16.1). Not the least of these is the emergence of the city–state as a dominant economic transactional unit. In today's world, mayors are just as likely as presidents or kings to initiate economic and cultural ties between distant lands. Another important and well-documented trend is the rapid opening of global markets, which is accompanied by a historic shift in the relative technological sophistication and wealth of nations. Global markets will continue to open as a result of vast political changes, such as those resulting from trade frictions between the United States and Japan or radical changes in national governments as are now going on in Eastern Europe. The acceleration of technological innovation (Brock & Hormats, 1990) is a third major trend (Figure 16.2), which explains the fact that approximately 90 percent of the scientists and engineers in the history of humankind are currently alive and active today (Wenk, 1986). These professionals account for the tremendous innovations that are at the core of the future technopolis. Still other trends in business, government, and science deserve more elaborate discussions.

Era of the Global Start-up

Today the world's telecommunications, transportation, and services delivery infrastructure is evolved to the extent that small, medium, and large companies alike are shaping their business strategy to capture global markets. As new levels of efficiency are achieved, the advantages of starting global businesses quickly outweigh the costs. As an example, the French high-tech medical company TechnoMed launched its business with one product to be delivered through four subsidiaries in the United States, Italy, Japan, and West Germany (Mamis, 1989). The company knew that their one product, a diagnostic imaging system, could compensate for its singularity by diversifying with respect to geography.

- Emergence of the city–state
- Globalization of markets
- Globalization of business, including start-ups
- Acceleration of technological innovation
- Internationalization of R&D
- Concern with intellectual property (sovereignty of nations)
- Burgeoning of the international service sector
- Increased and fluctuating demand for skilled labor
- Changing role of governmental intervention.

Figure 16.1. Economic and geopolitical trends.

Even those companies not started internationally are now extending through teaming agreements and joint ventures to acquire technology and tap global markets. Smaller, established U.S. companies not started internationally are now extending through teaming agreements and joint ventures to acquire technology and tap global markets. Smaller, established U.S. companies such as LSI Logic (Santa Clara, CA), an application-specific integrated circuits company, and Symbol Technologies (Binghampton, NY), in handheld bar code laser scanners, are developing their strengths internationally. These companies have improved their global competitive position by strategically buying and selling the technologies of their foreign partners while focusing on increasing market share. Globalization is at the core of their business strategy.

Internationalization of R&D

Small and large public and private, as well as profit and nonprofit, institutions are finding benefits from international linkages involving science and technology (Hladik & Linden, 1989). Whereas before such international linkages were focused primarily on manufacturing, distribution, and marketing, now these agreements are focused on R&D. The internationalization of research is being brought about through government-sponsored programs such as EUREKA as a part of the unification of the European market. R&D is being institutionalized through even broader initiatives such as the intelligent manufacturing mystem lead by Japan.

In some cases, whole industries, such as biotechnology, are characterized by the complex interweaving of R&D joint ventures, many devoted to product development. Such relationships will shape the character of the biotechnology industry in the future, making it a truly international industry.

Information Technology

Trend: Expanding economies of scale for the accumulation and use of information

Impact: Changing economies of scale in services and technology transfer; acceleration of innovation

New Materials

Trend: Swing away from exploitation of naturally occurring resources; trend toward human-made materials designed to fulfill a specific function

Impact: Intensified competition in many industries, (e.g., automotive, telecommunications, construction, and so forth)

Industrial Manufacturing

Trend: Industrial processes reoriented within a framework of computer-assisted design (CAD), computer-assisted manufacturing (CAM), and computer-integrated manufacturing (CIM)

Impact: Rapid change in the uses and need for human labor; flexibility and rapid adaptability of products to the benefit of producers and consumers

Transportation

Trend: Convergence of advances in information, materials, and manufacturing technologies to yield greater system efficiency

Impact: Dramatic linking of production centers and markets

Biotechnology

Trend: Ability to systematically alter biological forms

Impact: Near term agricultural and biomedical enhancements; major advances in diverse areas (e.g., materials processing, waste mangement, and computers)

Figure 16.2. Technological trends.

Regional disparities in scientific strengths and governmental regulations are also driving the internationalization of R&D. One example is the recent location of the major biotechnology research facility of BASF in Massachusetts (Wu & Lelyveld, 1990). This West German chemical giant located its research center in

Massachusetts to be near what BASF regarded as the finest scientific capability in the world with respect to its product development strategy. Anticipating the next step in this trend toward internationalization of R&D, the Japanese have already encouraged the United States and Europe to cooperate in the international computer linking of manufacturing capabilities (Mitsusada, 1989).

Emergence of the International Service Industry

Accompanying the internationalization of research and the trend toward global company formation is the rapid growth of international services to support these activities. Already, the major accounting firms have firmly established a global presence through mergers, acquisitions, and foreign offices. Parallel to their expansion has been the development of companies such as World Technology Executive Network, an international network of executives of high-tech companies that focuses on developing strategic alliances, partnerships, joint ventures, and equity participation for international firms in three U.S. and four European cities (Solomon, 1989). Regional governments are pursuing a similar strategy with the proliferation of programs that promise to link companies internationally for strategic partnering and joint ventures. Typically, these programs provide information that aggressive companies can eventually use to their advantage. Few regional-government-affiliated programs directly mold partnerships or business deals, nor do they consistently evaluate the results of their activities with respect to bottom-line business results.

Obviously, telecommunications is enhancing many of these international services, and in many, making them feasible. Texas Research and Technology Foundation in San Antonio obtains business translation services from a firm in Kansas City. In the process of providing a translation, first, second, and often third drafts are exchanged via telefax between San Antonio and Kansas City. Before the delivery of a finished product, the office in Kansas City double checks each draft of a translation by telefaxing the text for review by native speakers who actually reside in the foreign country. The price of this translation service conducted internationally is less than the cost of the same services if acquired in San Antonio.

Increased Fluctuating Demand for Skilled People

With the opening and expansion of global markets has come a rush to satisfy those markets with increased innovation and productive capacity. This in turn has resulted in an increased demand for skilled labor. No nation as of yet seems prepared to address this demand. Weaknesses in the U.S. educational system have resulted in a shortage of technologically trained workers, which ironically occurs at a time when the top 25 percent of our work force is among the best in the world. The report compiled Keidanren projects that Japan will experience a shortage of 200,000 technically skilled workers by 1993 (*Japan Times*, 1989).

One sees an increased mobility of skilled people, which is also driven by the demands placed by one country (i.e., the United States) on another (i.e., Japan). The U.S.-Japan Science Pact was to establish scholarships enabling international study by U.S. students abroad in Japan. As nations and companies alike recognize the origins of economic prosperity in early stage R&D, they are beginning to insist on equal access to the seeds of innovations in the universities and research centers of each other's countries (Narin & Frame, 1989).

Preoccupation with Intellectual Property and the Sovereignty of Nations

Now more than ever in the history of the world, ideas, their origin, value, transmittability, and protectability are shaping international relationships between nations and companies. These issues are also shaping international markets. It now costs as much as $100 million to develop a new drug but virtually nothing to copy that same drug once it is already developed. Unless countries can guarantee protection of intellectual property introduced into their markets, they are likely not to receive that product. And they will not receive the job-creating manufacturing facilities that would produce that product in their country. Today, intellectual property policy is shaping the future of countries such as Mexico, Brazil, Hong Kong, Indonesia, and Argentina. Until flaws in intellectual property policy and its enforcement are corrected in these countries, investments in R&D and technological preparation of the labor force will be wasted.

Changing Role of Governmental Intervention

This brings us to the complicated issue of intervention by those who would play a role of influencing international transactions in a global economy, specifically regional and national governments. If technology is the seed of economic prosperity, it follows that people and institutions will organize to develop and retain that value for themselves and their regions. Historically, the tools they had for capturing that value and translating it into economic growth and prosperity were based in regional governments or in national policy.

Today, with the emergence of a city–state and the internationalization of R&D, as well as its commercialization, it is impossible to know clearly for whom that value is to be retained and developed (*The Economist*, 1988). Yet the process continues. We hear frequently of cases where governments have regulated technology, not to protect the well-being of citizens or the environment, but to guard domestic markets for themselves. This regulation is evident in the recent struggle over high-density television. Some regulatory barriers to global markets are being diminished, for example, with the relaxation of restrictions imposed by the Coordinating Committee on Multilateral Export Control (COCOM) and corresponding COMECON in the Eastern Bloc.

Fluctuations and trends cannot be ignored by developers of smart global systems because they determine the size and accessibility of foreign markets. German environmentalists have been accused of forcing the German biotechnology industry out of that country by insisting on the strict regulation of manufacturing that involves recombinant DNA (Hudson, 1989). Because of the international concern over regulation, lobbying has become an international enterprise (Cregan, 1989) and will depend on a highly sophisticated infrastructure for the transmission of ideas and information. The globalization of companies questions the very nature of "What is a domestic industry?" If the technopolis is defined as a market-driven, nonregulating enabler of productive global transactions, these are some of the critical issues that the developers of the technopolis must consider.

IMPLICATIONS OF GLOBAL TRENDS FOR THE TECHNOPOLIS

There are at least five important implications of these trends that affect the developers of the technopolis and various components of a smart infrastructure (Figure 16.3):

1. *Increased importance of time and timing.* To the extent that the technopolis and smart infrastructure control and enhance the means of production or distribution, they control the time to market. In an information-based, technology-driven global economy, time to market is the most important competitive factor.
2. *Decreased importance of geographic proximity.* With significant efficiency gains in transportation and tremendous flexibility in the means of production, companies will not concern themselves with proximity to market as they have in the past, because virtually all markets are now accessible. Therefore, choices about where a company locates will depend more on the efficiencies afforded by the technopolis rather than geographic proximity to any resource.
3. *Expanding hinterlands.* In addition to linking centers globally through transportation, telecommunications, and other infrastructure systems, the technopolis can serve as a broader hinterland with information, services, and products. Hence each technopolis is tied differently than in the past to its hinterland and the markets it contains.
4. *Increasing importance of regional governments.* As it begins to draw on resources and take advantage from serving its surrounding region, the technopolis will depend increasingly on support and enabling activities of its local governments. This accompanies the emergence of the city–state.

- Increased importance of time and timing
- Decreased importance of geographic proximity
- Expanding hinterlands
- Changing role of regional governments
- Dependence on alliances, information, and services.

Figure 16.3. Implications of global trends for the technopolis.

5. *Dependence on alliances, information and services.* According to Peter Drucker (1989), business of the future will integrate themselves into the world economy through strategic alliances that take the form of minority participations, joint ventures, research and marketing consortia, partnerships, and special projects and cross-licensing arrangements. Businesses will rely on the technopolis and the smart infrastructure for the information and services to support these alliances.

TEXAS RESEARCH AND TECHNOLOGY FOUNDATION

Given these pervasive forces at work in our global economy, individuals, businesses, and even entire nations and regions within them are attempting to respond in a manner that ensures their economic competitiveness and maintains their quality of life. Concepts such as the technopolis, science city, research park, and technology incubator are favored tools for the organization of technological advances to better serve the economic needs of large populations. Texas Research and Technology Foundation (TRTF) is an example of a broad regional initiative organized and supported by the greater San Antonio community, which is seeking to prepare the economy of Texas, particuarly that of the San Antonio/Austin corridor, to adapt to the forces at work in our global economy. Early on, this organization recognized the importance of working internationally to create and retain economic value for the region.

TRTF Mission and Activities

TRTF is a not-for-profit organization established in 1984 as a science and technology economic developer serving Texas. The Foundation works with scientists and engineers of high-tech companies and research institutions to identify and develop research that holds high commercial potential. Around these results, TRTF seeks to form, finance, and support new companies, some of which will eventually reside in the Texas Research Park. The TRTF is first and foremost a technology-oriented service organization, accomplishing its mission through activities of its three operating divisions (Figure 16.4).

TRTF Structure

The organizing structure for TRTF represents an amalgam of the University City Science Center (Philadelphia), the oldest urban research park in the United States, and the Research Triangle Park (Raleigh–Durham). Hence, it combines a focus on value creation through company formation with aggressive efforts in facilities recruitment.

The TRTF is comprised of three operating divisions: Research and Development Division, Venture Division, and Research Park Division, which are supported and administered by a Corporate Services Division. The R&D Division creates consortially based research centers, develops and manages joint industry-institutional R&D programs, and recruits or retains scientists and entrepreneurs in Texas. The Venture Division actively forms and finances companies around technologies transferred from the R&D Division, as well as other research organizations. The Venture Division is the founding partner of VenTex, a for-profit company, which is now raising two venture capital funds for investment in technologies and new company formation. The Research Park Division is the manager and developer of the 1,500-acre Texas Research Park, located in the Texas Hill Country west of San Antonio. The Research Park Division is the developer of the University of Texas Institute of Biotechnology.

Serving and supporting the activities of these three operating divisions is the Corporate Services Division. Within this division, the administration and finance section administers the organization internal to TRTF and provides basic administrative services to client companies. The International Services Section

---

Mission: To develop the economy of Texas through science and technology

Activities:
- Creating and managing R&D programs with results of maximum commercial potential
- Actively forming new companies around technologies transferred from the research sector
- Providing the physical environment and facilities in the Texas Research Park for a community of scientists and entrepreneurs.

Figure 16.4. Texas Research and Technology Foundation (TRTF) mission and activities.

develops international joint ventures, manages international scientific exchange, and facilitates affiliations for reciprocal exchange among companies and research institutions of different nations. Finally, the National Security Section applies science and technology to the development of programs for defense industry preparedness and productivity.

TRTF INTERNATIONAL APPROACH

In recognition of the global technological, economic, and geopolitical trends that affect communities, as well as the businesses and individuals within them, the TRTF International Services Section is working with the businesses and research institutions of Texas to establish a strong presence in the global economy. This section provides international support services to the TRTF operating divisions and their clients. On behalf of these clients, TRTF International Services aims someday to manage the permanent presence of TRTF in Europe and the Far East. Through these operating divisions, TRTF provides the following services:

- Formation and management of joint ventures and strategic partnerships
- Development and management of programs for scientific exchange and technology transfer
- Establishment and management of the overseas corporate presence to enable expansion of foreign firms into North America.

Several specific programs have been initiated in partnership with other organizations around the world that contribute to these service abilities.[1]

International Ventures: STW/TRTF Cooperation

In 1989, TRTF established a cooperative agreement with the Steinbeis Foundation for Economic Development in Baden-Wuerttemberg, West Germany. The purpose of this agreement is to work on a reciprocal and mutually beneficial basis to transfer and commercialize technologies. The result of this activity will benefit the citizens and businesses of Texas and Baden-Wuerttemberg. STW was founded in 1971 to assist German companies with the broadest range of technology issues. Since its formation, STW has grown to include a network of 100 technology transfer centers around the state. These centers employ more than 2,000 people and include technical expertise in more than 100 disciplines relevant to the needs of industry.

International Infrastructure: World Research Park Consortium

In October 1989, leaders of twenty research parks representing eight of the developed nations met in Kyoto, Japan. They gathered to sign an agreement that created an international consortium of research parks devoting to promoting business transactions through the mutual marketing of research parks and the transfer of technology on an international basis (Figure 16.5). This consortium is currently developing its working protocols from assisting companies internationally who are seeking new technologies or to establish their international presence in foreign markets. The membership of the world research park consortium is working to form international joint ventures and strategic partnerships between companies. The World Research Park Consortium is also refering and assisting companies internationally for expansion and relocation.

International R&D: International Science
Exchange and Scholarship Program

Recognizing that the driving force in our global economy is human capital, the TRTF is developing mechanisms to enable the international exchange of scientists, entrepreneurs, and technicians. Toward this goal, TRTF seeks to form the International Science Exchange and Scholars Fund. Initially, that fund will be capitalized at $5 million, the interest from which will support activity within three program areas:

- International scientific exchange of research scientists among academic and basic research institutions
- Exchange of scientists among research institutions and the private sector to enable the acquisition of new skills or the diffusion of new technologies among those sectors of our economy where technology transfer is not currently likely to occur
- International scientific conference and information exchange program that will hold international conferences and develop publications that promote international scientific exchange.

The result of the fund will be that Texas is better able to recruit and retain high-quality scientists and researchers for the State of Texas and will benefit from an ever-expanding international network of scientists.

International Corporate Services:
Symmetrical Technology Exchange Project

TRTF recognizes the barriers confronting companies attempting to do business across international frontiers. These barriers may be structural barriers,

---

Purpose: To create an international consortium of research parks devoted to promoting business transactions through mutual marketing and technology transfer

Founded: October 1989 in Kyoto, Japan

Services/Programs:
- International Technology Business Incubator
- AsiaTex/EuroTex
- Formation of joint ventures and strategic partnerships
- Assistance in corporate expansion and relocation

Membership:
    12 in North America
     2 in Asia
     8 in Europe

Figure 16.5. World research park consortium.

which can be remedied by technological advances in fields such as telecommunications. They may also be governmentally imposed barriers, such as tariffs and regulations. Economic and financial barriers are created by the ever-changing dynamics of a global economy. Whatever the cause, such barriers inhibit the commercialization and diffusion of technology internationally and distort relationships that might otherwise be more reciprocal and mutually beneficial.

TRTF expects to develop the Symmetrical Technology Exchange Project (STEP), which will foster participation by American firms in those activities that ensure access to foreign markets. STEP will also support reciprocal international technology transfer through programs and other initiatives. Currently, STEP is recruiting a Euro-Info Center to North America. It is also establishing an international center for biotechnology and examining ways in which technical training can be conducted internationally to the mutual benefit of participating regions.

CONCLUSIONS

In conclusion, I am reminded of the observation by Edward Wenk, Jr., who explained how the United States has regrettably abandoned its railway system for national highways that have brought with them massive unanticipated maintenance and operational costs. In his essay he notes

The more massive a technology, the greater seems to be the political momentum for implementation and the greater the difficulty in identifying the trade-offs occasioned by its accomplishment. (1986, 38)

The technopolis is a massive technology. We see a growing momentum toward its global implementation. The promising advantages of the technopolis are still being identified and created. The trade-offs of using the technopolis are also yet to be identified.

The trends discussed in this chapter will certainly obviate these advantages and trade-offs. The globalization of business enterprise will cause us to reconsider our assumptions and business approaches to domestic markets. The internationalization of research and the resulting concern over intellectual property will redefine certain aspects of national sovereignty. The rules and responsibilities of governments will be changed by the mobility of skilled people and transmittability of goods and services, as well as the emergence of the city–state. All of this is brought about by gains in access and efficiency found in the technopolis. What is challenging for those of us who are developing the technopolis is the opportunity to develop programs, structures, and strategies that maximize the advantages afforded by technologies, while minimizing the trade-offs.

NOTES

1. The TRTF International Service Section was proposed to the TRTF trustees in 1990 in the form described here. The program as actually implemented is subject to change based on management decisions and other factors.

REFERENCES

Brock, W. E. & Hormats, R. D. *The Global Economy*. New York: The American Assembly, W. W. Norton, 1990.

Curran, D. J. & G. A. Lucci. "The ABCs of FTZs." *Business Age*, May 1989.

Dertouzos, M. L., R. K. Lester, R. M. Solow, & MIT Commission on Industrial Productivity. *Made in America—Regaining the Productive Edge*. Cambridge, MA: MIT Press, 1989.

Dobyns, N. L. "In This Us Versus Them World—Be Sure You Know Which is Which." Remarks made before the Washington International Business Council, November 6, 1987.

Drucker, P. "Peter Drucker's 1990s. "The Futures that Have Already Happened." *The Economist* (October 21), 1989.

Griffin, T. P. & C. M. Farr. "The FSX Debate: Implications for Future U.S. International Armaments Programs." *Program Manager* (July-August), 1989.

Hladik, K. J. & L. H. Linden. "Is An International Joint Venture in R&D for You?" *Research Technology Management* (July-August), 1989.

Hudson, R. L. "German Debate on Genes Stings Drug Makers." *Wall Street Journal*. (August 31), 1989.

Kean, T. H. "Boosting Small-Business Exports." *Issues in Science and Technology*, Spring 1989.

Malmgren, H. B. "Technology and the Economy." *The Global Economy*. New York: The American Assembly, W.W. Norton & Company, 1990.

Mamis, R. A. "Global Start-Up." *Inc.* (August), 1989.

Mitsusada, H. "Japan Seeks U.S., Europe Cooperation in Plan to Create Computer-Linked Factories." *The Japan Economic Journal* (July 15), 1989.

Narin, F. & J. D. Frame. "The Growth of Japanese Science and Technology." *Science*, vol. 245 (August), 1989.

Reichert, W. & H. Sello. "Whole-Earth Technology," *High Technology Business* (July-August), 1989.

Roman, D. D. & J. F. Puett, Jr. *International Business and Technological Innovation*, Elsevier Science Publishing Co., Inc., 1983.

Solomon, S. D. "Something of Value," *Inc.*, (July), 1989.

Staff Writer, "Whose Idea Is It Anyway?" *The Economist* (November 12), 1988.

Staff Writer, "Shortage of High-Tech Workers Seen by 1993." *The Japan Times* (July 15), 1989.

Weiss, T., ""Our Research is Being Sold for Bargain Prices," *Roll Call* (August 7-13), 1989.

Wenk, E., Jr. *Trade-offs—Imperatives of Choice in a High-Tech World*. Baltimore, MD: The Johns Hopkins University Press, 1986.

Wu, P. T. & M. Lelyveld. "BASF to Build Biotechnology Center in Mass." *Journal of Commerce* (January 23), 1990.

17

Culture and Entrepreneurial Success: Innovation in Science Parks

Dominique Fache

"Innovation is provocative to traditional culture." So said Karl Schumpeter in a statement implying also that the future should be elaborated out of a frozen, outdated, decaying past. Any creative process associated with destruction is bound to find its way through culture.

Culture should be as ambitious as economy, otherwise sclerosis would spread and the social body would dissolve. If we compare maps showing where economic success prevails with those showing where people are most creative, intelligent, and innovative—where culture in progress is most vivid—we see that there is a certain consistency, in history (Renaissance in Italy, Meiji Era in Japan), as well as in our modern world (California, northern Italy, Barcelona, and so forth).

Culture is no longer a by-product of an economical potential measured by purchasing capacity, nor the dying song of a civilization doomed to decadence. On the contrary, culture is the sign or even the necessary requirement of economic development, because strategic resources of a company do not lie only in capital or technology, but also in human capacities and adaptability.

Reverence for stability, meant to maintain comfortable operating conditions for the well-established mammoths of economy, is no longer in keeping with the strict requirements of competition. Linear management of occupied markets, controlled technology, and recurrent production methods lead companies to stagnation with no future. A quiet, immobile situation means death to economy.

It is essential to incorporate Schumpeter's "creative destruction" to revive uncertainty in our world of certitudes. This is the price to be paid for creating innovative conditions. This is also the part played by culture as a universal living spirit. Art and technology are bound together. Both express new ideas. Creativity includes risks, and therefore questions, therefore dialogue.

Such ideas do not fit exactly into the categories of traditional management. But it is to be found in the talk of some contemporary Japanese managers (such as Morita) illustrated by the fundamental concepts of the go-game Shuhari.

- Shu—absorb knowledge like a sponge
- Ha—select an original, therefore risky approach
- Ri—create bravely

In other words, we may consider the evolution of the Japanese model: the up-to-date motto Bi Kan you so (Beauty–pleasure–game–creativity). Such a philosophy supersedes both the big/thick/large/heavy descriptors of the 1950s and 1960s, and the small/light/narrow/thin descriptors of the 1970s and 1980s.

Finally, creativity pertains more to combinatory phenomena and fuzzy logics and integrates the complex and random elements that stop deductive reasoning. New prospects lie with unexpected alliances. The breakdown of partitions today allows for innovative breakthroughs in several fields.

Where is the link with the science park phenomenon? Up to now this concept has been understood as either a gadget for universities or politicians or an up-dated version of the "industrial area," meeting moral, esthetic, or fashion requirements accordingly or as a tool for implementing a development plan or a decentralization policy.

Development of the innovation process in science parks is hazardous and fragile. It needs much effort with little apparent result. Our experience shows that the success of an operation is basically a cultural one. Among all identifiable factors of success (good planning, management, location, link with universities, aggressive marketing, international networking, and a realistic financial approach), the cultural factor is probably the least considered because it is the most difficult to measure and to implement; it has to do with human attitudes, management of time, and social and cultural life.

Up to now the development of science parks in the world has been successful in terms of hardware (creating a new environment and better conditions to develop new products, new companies, and new sectors) and the status of the art in terms of hardware technology is well known. But one can observe that one can reach certain limits if one does not develop the software of the project, which is a cultural and sociological approach to the phenomenon.

How does culture affect business? This is a new challenge, creating a new model for the economy of the twenty-first century. The new possibilities offered by communication technologies (TV satellites, computer networks, and so forth) offer many new opportunities of exchange. This could be a great value from our European culture, especially around the Mediterranean Sea. Our Japanese partners also express this demand for their technopolis projects. Our technopolis concept, Sophia Antipolis, is now physically an adult, but I am not sure it has revealed all the possible resources in creativity.

Through a few examples, I will indicate some new ways of experimentation in this matter. The next step for the technopolis movement is to invest in culture as a worldwide common value, as a stimulus to exchange and creativity, and even as an integrated part of the worldwide economy. The technopolis must get the best of all traditions: Anglos-Saxon rigor, Japanese efficiency, and Latin management.

Considering various projects in the world and looking beyond brilliant material achievements, we are struck by conformity and a lack of daring spirit—by a wish for recognition from or conformity to existing models from an economic as well as building development point of view. These projects are places lured by the vertical integration of each field of technological development rather than by the horizontal grasp, transversality, and the overall integrated approach.

It is, however, highly probable that such an approach—closely related to the coming out of a worldwide economy and civilization—would be rich with creative, innovative elements. The urban cultural development (Paris, New York, and Berlin) is rapidly confronted with the authority of a highly organized market (shopping arcades, production circuits, museums, concert halls, and art circuits). In a network of science parks where the concept could be considered from the beginning in the general economic outline, it would have a different meaning of also participating in the overall profitability.

Now, let us take a few practical examples.

Environmental problems have recently proved vital for our societies. They concern every field of economic activity and the whole world. Clearly, new production methods, new products or technologies, and consumers' new requirements are generating a profitable market for the next twenty years. However, further to a worldwide consciousness, we should heavily invest in education, information, modelization, and research.

As philosophers, writers, and artists are busy expressing themselves, a new culture is arising. It would not only be an honor but also a wise investment for some science parks to dedicate themselves to some reflection and research on the subject. An international university for the environment, coordinating already existing means and abilities, could play a leading part, leaving aside the complicated implementation of government regulations.

Ethics and philosophy are becoming more integrated in all economic and technological development issues and not only in the biomedical field. New values and new behaviors are appearing. Modernity is not achieved only through new architectural forms or sophisticated technologies, but primarily by developing new concepts, new models, and new values meeting societies requirements. Companies and research centers do not provide meditation or contemplation rooms by chance, nor do big American business schools include art and ethics in their subjects by chance.

The confrontation of people, values, and cultures opens remarkable prospects for creativity and provides conditions for breakthroughs. New technologies in information, communication, and video allow for the development of quick, reliable systems giving access to knowledge and ideas that alone make progress possible. How far we are from the Coptic monk of a Cistercian abbey in the Middle Ages who nevertheless tried to fulfill the same role within the limitations of his time.

In the current innovation process we know how to duplicate the minimum technical data (building, technologies, scientific equipment, storage of existing knowledge, data collection, or technical training of people). What remains unexplained is the appearance of conditions for breakthrough thinking related to people's characters and interaction with the environment. How best to take advantage of the interaction to create the conditions for the rise of a daring entrepreneurial spirit beyond the factual opportunities of markets and techniques?

The answer, to me, is to bet on culture. This seems to me to be the only lasting security for a renewed growth. However, we must be aware of the difficulty of loose measurements that cannot be appreciated in known scales and methods. The analysis of the investment return can hardly be scheduled or demonstrated except by example.

Yet, if I were asked today to advise a country, or a region, or a university already having or planning a technopolis, I would say, "Place a priority on culture." Gather up your resources in this respect, create places where people can meet and talk, build a "think tank" to your scale in various fields—a Villa Medicis or Barbariga, a Gulbenkian or Maeght Foundation, a small Beaubourg, a new Bauhaus, a Mass Moca as in North Adams, and so forth.

Bring together thinkers, creators, plasticians, musicians, artists, and scientists from everywhere. Get local people interested and attract other partners (industries, banks, and public bodies). If possible, take the university as a partner so that it can develop new prospects of its own. Create one or several national or international events (Davos seminars, round tables, festivals, Bichat talks, Rome clubs, and so forth). Set up a library; encourage clubs; organize concerts, exhibitions, seminaries, conferences, and workshops; and integrate the policy in the general outline, investments, and management. And do it in harmony with your community, using or boosting local resources. Of course, the other success ingredients should not be overlooked; their efficiency is considerably increased in such contexts.

To implement this policy needs daring spirit, open-mindedness, a strong character capable of imposing ideas; and a pluridisciplinary team to imagine, administrate, manage, and stimulate the project. There are no noble tasks and lowly tasks; the engineer and the artist should be reconciliated to the advantage of both. It is a question of determination in implementing the policy and a question of timing. Ambitions should be made clear from the beginning if they are to allow for better marketing and also for creating the style and originality of the project.

The cultural bet is more integrated in the business world, including what is required to form managerial staff. The technopolis concept can find there a second wind directed toward better creativity and operational efficiency; it can also be a "pilot of modernity" in our societies.

We must cultivate what will become the most precious and rare materials of the twenty-first century. These will be neither energy, space, nor capital but imagination, creativity, and intelligence. We cannot prepare for this revolution of intelligence without culture. After reading Leonardo da Vinci's notes, I discovered that he was the true father of the technopolis.

18

The Multimedia City of the Future

Sheridan M. Tatsuno

It is September 2007. Your six-year-old daughter has returned home from school and persuaded you to take her on a quick study tour of the Louvre for a class assignment. You put on your "virtual reality" TV helmet and skim through the museum's visual catalogue. Her assignment is seventeenth-century French artists. You say "Seventeenth-century—Georges de la Tour" into the speaker. Immediately, you are taken on a 3-D simulated tour of the Louvre by a renowned art historian who stops before painting, "Saint Joseph in the Carpenter's Shop, 1640." As you both gaze at a painting, your daughter calls her friend on the videophone and they edit the picture and swap ideas for their joint school project. You marvel at your daughter's technical wizardry. She has mastered image editing. . . . Welcome to the multimedia city of the future.

During the past decade, we have witnessed an explosion of new information technologies that are dramatically reshaping the way we live and think. The personal computer, the facsimile machine, the videotape recorder, and the cellular phone are redefining the way we do business and communicate with each other. George Gilder (1989) calls this the "Era of the Microcosm." Like the telephone and the airplane, these electronic devices have become the new engines of economic growth. They are shrinking distances, costs, and time. But this is only the beginning. The pace of technological change is accelerating. Soon, we will be inundated by a new wave of high-definition TVs, interactive computers, pocket phones, and desktop supercomputers that will reshape our communities and cities. Our children, already raised on a steady diet of television and Nintendo video games, are absorbing these technologies at a phenomenal rate. Only parents and teachers are unable to keep up with the times, yet these are the people making decisions about our future. How will we prepare ourselves for this frenetic change? What is multimedia? And how will it influence the way our cities develop? This chapter examines the evolution of postwar cities and the emergence of the "multimedia city" of the future.

THE AGE OF TECHNOPOLIS

Since World War II, we have witnessed a rapid decentralization of cities. As shown in Table 18.1, prewar seaports, railports, and company towns were rigid pyramidal structures dominated by an economic elite of "city fathers." Like their corporate counterparts, these cities centralized power and treated their citizens like political pawns. There was little real democracy, especially for the disenfranchised poor and minority. Corporate leaders and politicians tightly controlled the distribution of information, jobs, and services.

During the postwar era, the pyramidal power structure has rapidly eroded. Medium- and high-tech industries have dispersed people, jobs, and political power to the suburbs. Downtown areas are becoming impoverished and multiculturally diverse as new immigrants replace the departing middle class. Central cities, once centers of economic and political power, are now being challenged by suburban governments. Although urban problems are increasingly regional in scope, cities are suffering from political "gridlock" because of their unwillingness to work together to resolve these overlapping problems. They are still mimicking the power-elite notions of the past.

As the twentieth century closes, major cities are undergoing a rapid metamorphosis. The great city–states of the past are declining. They have been joined by high-tech regions such as Silicon Valley, Sophia Antipolis, and the

Table 18.1. Technology and the Evolving Urban Landscape

Pre–1950	1960–1990	1990 and beyond
Seaports and railports	Airports and technopolises	Teleports and mediaports
Heavy industries	High-tech industries	"Humanware" industries
Low-value-added services	Medium-value-added services	High-value-added services
Central city	Suburbanization	Multinodal networked cities
Company towns	High-tech suburbs	Global villages
Centralized power	Dispersed power	Interactive power
Monocultural	Multicultural	Cultural fusion

Hsinchu Science City, which are clustering around airports and research universities. The new wealth of nations is no longer determined by access to raw materials and sealanes, but by brainpower, airports, and rapid communications. This shift to high technology is creating the high-tech suburban research park, or technopolis. Like the postwar suburbs of the 1950s and 1960s, the technopolis is an extension of existing cities. It is a concentration of brainpower around the new sources of wealth. However, unlike older cities, technopolises lie outside the mainstream of urban change. Unlike the middle-class suburb, the technopolis is a community of technocratic elites who have little in common with existing cities. They often live in total geographic and psychological isolation from the average urban dweller. Indeed, the technopolis as now envisaged may be a viable option, but it is not a solution for major urban problems in the twenty-first century. New emerging metaphors are needed to revitalize major cities around the world.

THE RISE OF GLOBAL NETWORK CITIES AND INTELLIGENT CITIES

One emerging metaphor is the global network city (Figure 18.1). Cities are now becoming clusters of dispersed economic nodes linked by massive networks of airports, highways, and communications. No longer dependent on central cities, these global network cities are like personal computers. They are highly interactive, flexible, and rapid. They thrive on networking, information swapping, and power sharing, not top-down, centralized management and control. Their competitive edge comes from focusing on high-value-added industries, such as design services, genetic engineering, supercomputing, and new materials research, which are increasingly being pursued by entrepreneurs and start-up companies. Unlike the technology-oriented technopolis, global network cities are more concerned about linkages and networking. Their value comes from the rapid exchange and transformation of raw information into highly valuable knowledge. In short, they are "knowledge processors."

Another metaphor is the intelligent city, which features advanced information and communications technologies to add value to everyday urban activities (Figure 18.1). For example, an intelligent city might feature a business complex of intelligent buildings wired with fiber-optic cables and outfitted with communications satellite antennas. Unlike the more open global network city, intelligent cities are closed systems. They often develop around corporations that used closed-circuit systems to protect their proprietary know-how. Although open public systems can be introduced, high infrastructure costs usually mean that the private sector are the major users and beneficiaries.

Thus, global network cities and intelligent cities are economically efficient, but they are rooted in the social structures of the past. Essentially, they are social pyramids—"electronic fortresses"—ruled by a technocratic elite. Like the ancient Greek city–states, these cities are divided into information "haves" and "have-nots."

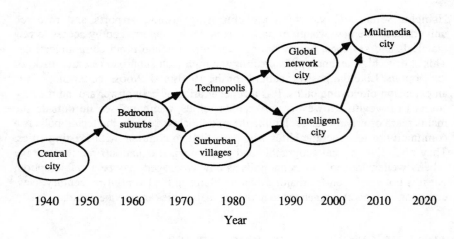

Figure 18.1. Emerging urban metaphors.

Those with access to the best education and networked databases have the greatest financial and political power; the have-nots remain ignorant, homeless, and hungry. In existing cities, information has not become an equalizer and leveler, but a social barrier. Moreover, despite their multicultural flavor, global network cities tend to be controlled by dominant cultures. New York City, Rio de Janeiro, and London are largely Eurocentric cities that overlook the majority of newcomers from non-European nations. In Asia, cities like Singapore and Manila are heavily dominated by Chinese financial elites. Almost without exception, the have-nots lack the access to information that could measurably improve their lives. Information processing, or learning, remains largely a personal activity that is left to private industry and market dynamics. Although this market-driven approach rewards entrepreneurialism, it shuts out those who are handicapped by physical disability, race, religion, or sex.

THE MULTIMEDIA CITY AS ELECTRONIC MOSAIC

During the twenty-first century, control over information and knowledge will become a major focus of political debate. It will determine the shaping of our emerging urban networks. How can people be educated, especially the poor and illiterate? How can they gain access to the crucial information that will help them find jobs, housing, and services? Recently, a United Nations' population report warned that the world's population, now 5.3 billion, will increase by 100 million annually during the 1990s. Nafis Sadik, executive of the UN Population Fund states: "The next ten years will decide the shape of the 21st century. They will decide whether the pace of damage to the environment speeds up or slows down...

The best and quickest way to reduce population growth will be to invest in improving women's status, access to education, health, and access to family planning."

In the coming population explosion, the technopolis as now envisaged remains outside the mainstream of these massive urban changes. How can information technologies be used to address the critical issues of family planning, health, education, jobs, and transportation? How can information be made accessible, easy to use, appropriate, and inexpensive? How can it be used to make our cities more equitable and human friendly? These are the key challenges facing policy planners, government and industry leaders, and city officials around the world.

One possible scenario is the multimedia city, a global networked city in which information is pushed down the social pyramid to the poorest person. It is not just a high-tech media city like Hollywood or Silicon Valley, but also a low-tech, high-touch city like Bangalore, New York's Harlem, or Lima's barrios. Indeed, the ultimate multimedia city is not a place but a state of mind. It is a city in which information is easily accessible to the average person. What is multimedia? And how might it be used in the future?

Multimedia is a combination of hardware and software technologies that involves the use of the six human senses in working, learning, and entertainment (Figure 18.2). It is a way of making machines easier to use and "human-friendly." Multimedia machines would feature image, voice, and touch sensors, keyboards, and "intelligent skins" to capture information from the user and communicate with others. Interactive multimedia TVs, for example, would allow students to navigate through art museums and science libraries. In Japan, Gifu City has developed a high-definition television (HDTV) "Hi-Vision" art gallery that enables visitors to choose narrated documentaries of painters and sculptors. In a study booth, art students can explore various painters and works of art by clicking through the menus of a personal computer equipped with a color monitor. Multicultural CD-ROM libraries could provide information and images everything from Indian sutras to Irish ballads for our increasingly multicultural cities.

In poorer nations, inexpensive color TVs can be linked to communications satellites that broadcast educational programs on farming, health care, math, and science. Mainland China is exploring these options. A farmer seeking advice on the best crops to grow without using chemicals, for example, could click into an interactive database on future pricing trends and organic growing practices. Usually the center of research activity, the city would become a repository of on-line information. One system currently in operation is Holland's computerized flower auction, in which members of a flower cooperative can log into on-line databases that provide up-to-date flower pricing trends and market demand. Flower growers can plant and sell the exact types and amount of flowers for each season. This computerized system is eliminating the need for bidders to attend the flower auction center and has dramatically increased profit margins and has reduced waste. This system would be useful for transporting perishable foods in tropical climates.

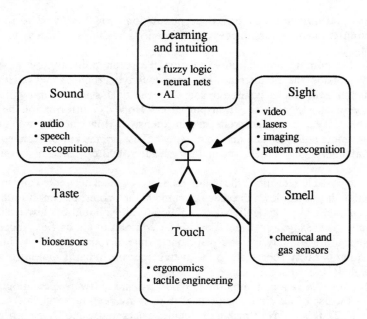

Figure 18.2. Multimedia technologies.

What makes multimedia so challenging is its unlimited possibilities. Unlike past technological revolutions, multimedia technologies will require a new way of thinking. Breakthroughs will not come from linear extrapolation of single technologies, but from the fusion of many technologies developed by multidisciplinary teams of policy makers, companies, and citizens. Moreover, useful applications will involve multifunctional, multisensory, and multicultural software. Multimedia study centers, for example, might use heads-up displays, sensory panels, expert systems, and interactive video technologies. Simple interactive TVs for poor farmers might be limited to voice recognition speakers, touch pads, and satellite uplinks. Fishermen could call into weather forecasting and fish pricing databases from handheld computer terminals anywhere at sea. Pioneers in this field will be leaders in "humanware" engineering—designing technologies around human aspirations and needs.

The multimedia city of the future could take a variety of forms (Table 18.2). In the field of education, schools could work with public libraries to coordinate curriculum development and establish multimedia centers with interactive personal computers and on-line software. For example, students could study using interactive software, then take a test to identify areas requiring further work. People changing careers could determine the requirements for obtaining a credential in another field, then study the curriculum on CD-ROM discs. For senior citizens or

Table 18.2. Multimedia City Types

Type	Major Applications	Technologies
Education	Interactive learning centers	Multimedia computers
Entertainment	Big-screen video bars/restaurants	High-definition TV
Social services	Medical on-line information	"Minitel"videotext
Cultural	International art collections	CD-ROM libraries
Leisure/resorts	Preview tours	Laser disc libraries
Business support	Software training	Interactive training
Commercial retail	Yellow pages	Videotext cable TV
Manufacturing	Just-in-time delivery	Computer networks
Utilities	Monthly billing information	Phone inquiry services
Sports	Football, baseball, basketball	Large stadium monitors
Environment	Pollution monitoring	Sensor networks

people in rural areas, mobile multimedia study centers could be developed. Eventually, most people will want their own portable learning centers. They could be supported by tax policies, such as Individual Training Accounts (ITAs).

Traffic reporting and government services are two fields that would benefit from advanced multimedia approaches. Commuters, for example, could avoid traffic jams by turning on interactive TVs that show sections of highways and roads. A driver could indicate the planned commuting route and see possible tie-ups enroute. Tokyo and Los Angeles, for example, have developed a traffic system that enables controllers to route cars around accidents and construction areas. At city offices, people inquiring about business license requirements, zoning codes, or property taxes could ask questions to a computerized database. Fuzzy logic, an emerging technology that can distinguish between shades of meanings and can thus enable machines to recognize voices, could allow computers to be linked directly to the telephone.

Business support is critical for attracting and retaining "foot-loose" companies, especially global high-tech corporations. A major challenge facing all corporations is the lack of highly qualified, trained workers. U.S. corporations, for example, reportedly spend more than $200 billion annually to train and retrain its work force. Cities could assist in improving their global competitiveness by opening multimedia training centers equipped with interactive computers, videotape and CD-ROM libraries, and on-line database services. Unemployed workers, for example, could have their skills assessed by computer, then receive a printout of potential jobs or careers that could use their talents. The skills assessment would not only include reading and writing skills, but also mechanical aptitude, image recognition, personal relations, and organizational abilities. Guided curriculum could be developed by local schools and colleges in collaboration with companies and industry associations.

Protecting the urban environment is a growing concern, especially among the middle class and poor who are most affected by worsening pollution. A multimedia city would feature an integrated pollution detection network to monitor smog levels and the presence of toxic wastes. These systems could be linked to hospitals and public health clinics that would warn people about hazardous activities to avoid. More preventive measures might include educating citizens to become more environmentally friendly through radio, television, and schools. Interactive on-line databases, for example, could answer questions and offer practical advice on household cleansers, high power line emissions, and indoor home pollution.

MULTIMEDIA CITY EXPERIMENTS

Multimedia is not only a dream of visionaries; it has become experimental systems in Japan and the United States. There are a handful of cities exploring the use of HDTV and computers to address the social needs described earlier (Table 18.3). In Japan, city governments are developing multimedia cities via HDTV, while U.S. cities are pursuing personal computer technologies. What are these cities doing?

Since unveiling high-definition television during the 1988 Olympics, the Ministry of Posts and Telecommunications (MPT) and the Ministry of International Trade and Industry (MITI) have introduced two competing multimedia programs: MPT's Hi-Vision Cities Program and MITI's Hi-Vision Communities Program. In April 1989, MPT selected 18 hi-vision cities from 71 competing sites to promote the use of HDTV in government offices, schools, public malls, hospitals, and museums. The $110 million program is being financed through the Japan Development Bank and Hokkaido North East Development Bank with direct investments, low-interest and no-interest loans, and tax incentives. Under a 1989 tax revision, these cities also qualify for tax exemptions. In early 1990, MITI selected six Hi-Vision Communities of its own. The following is a brief description of seven hi-vision cities:

The Gifu Museum outside of Nagoya city has invested in HDTV equipment to show short historical documentaries about famous painters and sculptors. The Hi-Vision Gallery, seating 75 people, features a 15-foot rear-projection screen, which runs eight programs on CD-ROMs. A smaller hi-vision picture frame offers showings for groups of four to six people. The hi-vision study booth allows art students and other researchers to browse through selected works of arts. The HDTV equipment has increased museum attendance and drawn a broader audience. Currently, the museum is building a CD-ROM art library in cooperation with museums in the United States, Europe, and Asia.

**Table 18.3. Leading Multimedia City Activities
in Japan and the United States**

Location	Multimedia Experiments
Gifu, Japan	HDTV art gallery
Hiroshima, Japan	International Hi-vision convention hall
Kawasaki, Japan	Downtown Hi-vision optical network
Chiba, Japan	Hi-vision cultural center
Hachioji, Japan	Children's Hi-Vision Science Museum
Cupertino, California	Multimedia Education Center
Los Angeles, California	Vivarium Project (Alan Kay, Apple Computer)
San Francisco, California	Multimedia software "capital" south of Market Street
Pittsburgh, Pennsylvania	Carnegie-Mellon University's AI Research Center
Santa Monica, California	Government service on-line network

Kita-Kyushu City is offering live HDTV broadcasts of its Space World Exposition to sister cities in Dalien, China; Tacoma, Washington; Inchon, Korea; Norfolk, Virginia; and the University of Pennsylvania. City officials are studying the possibility of a hi-vision museum using an integrated digital network service (ISDN) infrastructure and broadcast satellites to link up with its sister cities and Tokyo.

Hiroshima is positioning itself as "Hollywood East." In October, the city held a Hi-Vision City '89 Symposium with leading filmmakers to display HDTV movies at its new 37-foot screen in the international convention hall. In the summer of 1990, Hiroshima will hold its third International Animation Festival to explore HDTV as a tool for promoting world peace. More than 400 animation artists from around the world will show their videos. HDTV courses at a technical college are also being planned.

Kawasaki City, which is located between Tokyo and Yokohama, has developed an ambitious strategic HDTV city plan to introduce an HDTV fiber-optics network linking government, business, public, and office facilities.

Hachioji City outside of Tokyo installed a 90-inch HDTV set in its Children's Science Museum. Because of a shortage of video programming, the city holds an annual Big West Video Festival and Campus Art Hi-Vision Program and plans to exchange videodiscs, satellite programs, and HDTV tapes with other Japanese cities.

Sakai, a small industrial town near Osaka, is exploring HDTV as a tool to help heavy waterfront industries and small businesses shift into higher value-added manufacturing and services. The city is planning a Hi-Vision Plaza featuring an

HDTV museum, library, and information system linked to the South Osaka Regional Industrial Promotion Center, downtown offices, shopping malls, and local colleges.

The United States is also pursuing activities that will form the basis for the multimedia city of the future. Apple Computer, for example, recently opened a Multimedia Education Center in Cupertino to explore and develop new multimedia software for local schools. Traditional lectures and textbooks have been replaced by group projects and interactive computer learning. In east Los Angeles, computer guru Alan Kay is heading Apple's Vivarium Project, an experiment in artificial intelligence for grade school children. Children work on personal computers built into round tables, which allow them to create lifelike fantasy scenarios such as creating underwater animals that respond to their commands. At the university level, MIT's Media Lab and Carnegie-Mellon's artificial intelligence research center are developing new multimedia systems and software for future machines. Among entrepreneurs, San Francisco is rapidly shaping up as the capital of multimedia software because of its proximity to Silicon Valley and concentration of talented artists, software programmers, and designers. MacroMind, creator of the Multimedia Director Program, is one of the leading software company in this field. There is great deal of excitement over prospects of the 1990s becoming the decade of multimedia computing, just as the 1980s was the decade of personal computing.

MAKING THE MULTIMEDIA CITY A REALITY

Ultimately, the key to the successful of multimedia cities will be the usefulness and cost of their systems. Are the multimedia systems being developed useful? And are they affordable for the average person? Unless these two conditions are met, the multimedia city of the future will remain just a visionary dream. Policy makers can assist in making multimedia cities a reality by encouraging citizens and companies to participate in developing these new systems. There are various policy options that can be pursued through the efforts of public-private partnerships. For example, city officials could

- Establish multimedia education centers to develop new educational curriculum
- Encourage government funding of university multimedia centers to develop software for local schools, medical clinics, and government agencies
- Establish a National Multimedia Information Network linked to fiber-optic cables and broadcast satellites
- Encourage leading companies to establish multimedia contests for outstanding software and novel experiments
- Hold international multimedia city conferences to invite top researchers and users to share their experiences

- Develop long-term multimedia city plans to link emerging needs in education, energy, finance, environmental protection, technology, and transportation
- Establish public and privte sector ITAs to promote self-education, self-training, and self-management.

By becoming more forward-looking, urban policy makers can harness critical new technologies to solve problems of poverty, unemployment, illiteracy, poor health, traffic, and crime. In new technologies, it is usually not the most complex and expensive system that wins, but the most inexpensive and easy-to-use solution. The multimedia city of the future would accelerate the process of technology diffusion. It would be a global learning network in which the best ideas and solutions are rapidly conveyed through the network.

REFERENCES

Brand, S. *The Media Lab: Inventing the Future at M.I.T.* New York: Viking Penguin, Inc., 1987.

Davis, D. B. "Intel and IBM Share Their Multimedia Vision." *Electronic Business,* November 13, 1989, pp. 26–30.

Ditlea, S. "Inside Artificial Reality." *PC/Computing*, November 1989, pp. 91–102.

Gilder, G. *Microcosm: The Quantum Revolution in Economics and Technology.* New York: Simon & Schuster, 1989.

Hi-Vision City Concept Committee. *Hi-Vision City.* Tokyo: Nikkan Kogyo Shimbun (Japan Industrial Newspaper), July 1988.

Miller, M. W. "Digital Revolution: Vast Changes Loom as Computers Digest Words, Sounds, Images." *Wall Street Journal* (June 7), 1989, p. 1.

Sculley, John. "A Twenty-First Century Renaissance." *Odyssey.* New York: Harper & Row, 1987.

Shao, M. and R. Brandt. "It's a PC, It's a TV—It's Multimedia." *Business Week* (October 9), 1989, pp. 152–166.

Smilor, R. W., G. Kozmetsky, & D. V. Gibson. *Creating the Technopolis,* New York: Ballinger, 1988.

Stover, D. "Hypermedia," *Popular Science* (May), 1989, pp. 122–124.

Tatsuno, S. M. "High-Definition Television: The Next-Generation Video Battlefield." *Created in Japan.* New York: Harper & Row, 1989.

Ward, F. "Images for the Computer Age." *National Geographic* (June), 1989, pp. 720–751.

About the Editors

David V. Gibson is associate director, Center for Technology Venturing, College and Graduate School of Business and a senior research fellow at the IC² Institute at the University of Texas at Austin. He received his B.A. from Temple University in 1969, an M.A. from Pennsylvania State University in 1971, and an M.A. and Ph.D. from Stanford University in 1983 after completing studies in the areas of organizational behavior and communication theory.

Dr. Gibson is co-director of the Multidisciplinary Technology Transfer Research Group at the University of Texas. He teaches undergraduate and graduate courses on communication behavior in organizations, international business, technology transfer, the management of technology and information systems, and research methods. He belongs to the following professional associations: the Academy of Management, the American Sociological Association, the International Communication Association, and TIMS ORSA (College on Innovation Management and Entrepreneurship).

Dr. Gibson's research and publications focus on the management of information systems, cross-cultural communication and management, and technology transfer. He has published in the *Journal of Business Communications, Journal of Business Venturing, Journal of Engineering and Technology Management, IEEE Transactions in Engineering Management, Research Technology Management, Journal of Technology Transfer, Technology in Society,* and *Journal of Organizational Computing.* Dr. Gibson is a consultant to business and government and has made professional and keynote presentations in France, Ireland, Italy, England, Egypt and Taiwan. He is coeditor of *Creating the Technopolis: Linking Technology Commercialization and Economic Development* (Ballinger, 1988), *Technology Transfer: A Communication Perspective* (Sage, 1990), *University Spin-Off Companies: Economic*

Development, Faculty Entrepreneurs, and Technology Transfer (Rowman & Littlefield, 1991); editor of *Technology Companies and Global Markets: Programs, Policies, and Strategies to Accelerate Innovation and Entrepreneurship* (Rowman & Littlefield, 1991); and coeditor of *Technology Transfer in Consortia and Strategic Alliances* (Rowman & Littlefield, 1992).

George Kozmetsky is executive associate for Economic Affairs, the University of Texas System, director of IC^2 Institute, and the J. Marion West Chair Professor at the University of Texas at Austin, and professor in the Department of Medicine of the University of Texas Health Science Center at San Antonio. Dr. Kozmetsky served from 1966 to 1982 as dean of the College of Business Administration and the Graduate School of Business at the University of Texas at Austin. He received a B.A. from the University of Washington in 1938, an M.B.A. in 1947, and a Ph.D. in Commercial Science in 1957 from Harvard University.

His business acumen spans service, manufacturing, and technology-based industries. He is the cofounder, a director, and former executive vice president of Teledyne, Inc. He serves on the boards of several other companies. He is an acknowledged expert in high technology and venture capital.

Dr. Kozmetsky is a fellow of the American Association for the Advancement of Science. He is a charter member and served as president of the Institute of Management Sciences (TIMS). He also is a chancellor of the American Society for Macro-Engineering and president of the Large-Scale Programs Institute. He serves as a special reviewer for the National Science Foundation and is a member of the American Institute of Certified Public Accountants and the British Interplanetary Society.

Dr. Kozmetsky has served both state and federal governments as an advisor, commissioner, and panel member of various task forces, commissions, and policy boards. He regularly provides special testimony on business and technology issues to state and federal legislators.

Dr. Kozmetsky's articles and papers have appeared in major professional journals, magazines, and newspapers. His two most recent books are *Transnational Management* (Ballinger, 1985), and *Financing and Managing Fast Growth Companies: The Venture Capital Process* (Lexington, 1985).

Raymond W. Smilor is vice president of the Center for Entrepreneurial Leadership at the Ewing Kauffman Foundation in Kansas City, Missouri. He also holds the Ewing Kauffman Chair Professor in Entrepreneurship at the Bloch School of Business at the University of Missouri at Kansas City.

Dr. Smilor has published extensively with refereed articles appearing in journals such as *IEEE Transactions on Engineering Management, Research/Technology Management, Journal of Business Venturing,* and *Journal of Technology Transfer.* He is an associate editor for the department of R&D/Innovation and Entrepreneurship in Management Science. His research and consulting areas include technology transfer, entrepreneurship, economic development, and technology management and marketing. His works have been translated into Japanese, French, and Russian. He is past chairman of the College on Innovation Management and Entrepreneurship of the Institute of Management Sciences.

Dr. Smilor is the author or editor of *Corporate Creativity* (Praeger, 1984), *Financing and Managing Fast Growth Companies: The Venture Capital Process* (Lexington, 1985), *The Art and Science of Entrepreneurship* (Ballinger, 1987), *The New Business Incubator* (Lexington, 1986), *Creating the Technopolis* (Ballinger, 1988), *Customer-Driven Marketing: Lessons from Entrepreneurial Technology Companies* (Lexington, 1989), *University Spin-Off Companies* (Rowman & Littlefield, 1991), and *Technology Transfer in Consortia and Strategic Alliances* (Rowman & Littlefield, 1992).

Dr. Smilor is a consultant to business and government. He has lectured internationally in China, Japan, Canada, England, France, Italy, and Australia. He is an adjunct professor of Entrepreneurial Studies at the School of Business, Bond University in Australia, and a member of the Scientific Committee for the Advanced School for Managing Innovation and Technology in Bari, Italy. He is a featured presenter in many national and international conferences.

Contributors

Howard E. Aldrich
Professor of Sociology and
 Adjunct Professor of Business
 Administration
University of North Carolina
Chapel Hill, North Carolina

David Alan Aschauer
Senior Economist
Federal Reserve Bank of Chicago
Chicago, Illinois

Umberto Bozzo
Director General
Tecnopolis CASTA
Valenzano-Bari, Italy

Stewart Brand
Global Business Network
Sausalito, California

Mary Ann von Glinow
Graduate School of Business
 Administration
University of Southern California
Los Angeles, California

Pleasantine Drake
Architectural Diagnostics
Center of Building Diagnostics
 (CAN TECH) Ltd.
Ottawa, Canada

Sten Engelstoft
FAST Research Fellow
Commission of the European
 Communities
Brussels, Belgium

Dominique Fache
Consultant
Sophia-Antipolis
Valboune, France

Richard W. Morris
Vice President and Executive
 Associate to the President
Texas Research and Technology
 Institute
San Antonio, Texas

Volker Hartkopf
Center for Building Performance
 and Diagnostics
Carnegie Mellon University
Pittsburgh, Pennsylvania

Bob Hodgson
Director
Segal Quince Wickstead Ltd.
 Cambridge, England

James Hudak
Partner
Andersen Consulting
San Francisco, California

Vivian Loftness
Center for Building Performance
 and Diagnostics
Department of Architecture
Carnegie Mellon University
Pittsburgh, Pennsylvania

Regis McKenna
Chairman
Regis McKenna, Inc.
Palo Alto, California

Gerhard O. Mensch
Director
4IN International Institute
 of Industrial Innovations
Munich, Federal Republic of Germany

Peter A. D. Mill
President
Center of Building Diagnostics
(CAN TECH) Ltd.
Ottawa, Canada

Viacheslav D. Pis'menny
Director
Troitsk Branch of the Kurchatov
 Institute
Kurchatov Atomic Energy
 Institute
Moscow, USSR

Jerry Richardson
Principal
Richardson Associates
San Francisco, California

W. W. Rostow
Professor Emeritus of Political
 Economy
Department of Economics
University of Texas at Austin
Austin, Texas

Sheridan M. Tatsuno
Principal
NeoConcepts
Fremont, California

Michael H. Wakelin
Manager
Marketing and Project
 Development
Bechtel Civil Company
San Francisco, California

Frederick Williams
Professor
College of Communications
University of Texas at Austin
Austin, Texas

About the Sponsors

The IC² Institute, The University of Texas at Austin is a major international research center for the study of Innovation, Creativity and Capital—hence IC². The institute studies and analyzes the enterprise system through an integrated and multidisciplinary program of research, conferences, and publications and directs the activities of more than 80 research fellows. IC² links theory with practice by bringing together business, government, and academic leaders through an active, international program of conferences, workshops, and colloquia.

The Bechtel Group, Inc. is a professional engineering and construction firm headquartered in San Francisco with global regional branches. Bechtel provides premier technical and management services to develop, manage, engineer, build, and operate installations and perform other related services to improve the standard of living and quality of life worldwide.

The RGK Foundation was established in 1966 to provide support for medical and educational research. It has sponsored studies and conferences in several areas of national and international concern, including health, corporate governance, energy, and economic analysis. Conferences sponsored at the Austin-based foundation are designed not only to enhance information exchange, but also to maintain an interlinkage among business, academia, community, and government.

Arthur Andersen and Co., Société Coopérative, is a professional services organization that serves clients through two business units—Arthur Andersen, which offers audit, tax, and financial consulting services and Andersen Consulting, which offers information consulting and technology solutions. As a global professional services organization, Arthur Andersen brings worldwide resources to bear on the rapidly changing needs of individual clients.